The
Modern
Christian Mystic

The Modern Christian Mystic

Finding the Unitive Presence of God

Albert J. LaChance, PhD

WITH A FOREWORD BY
CAROL WALLAS LACHANCE, MED

A POEM BY
PAUL WEISS

AND AN AFTERWORD BY
REV. SARAH ROBBINS-COLE, MA

North Atlantic Books
Berkeley, California

Published by
North Atlantic Books
P.O. Box 12327   Cover photo © Mikdam/Dreamstime
Berkeley, California 94712   Cover and book design by Susan Quasha

Printed in the United States of America

The poem "You Hold This" on page 132 is reproduced by permission of Paul Weiss, copyright © 2007 by Paul Weiss.

The Modern Christian Mystic: A Unitive Approach to the Presence of God is sponsored by the Society for the Study of Native Arts and Sciences, a nonprofit educational corporation whose goals are to develop an educational and crosscultural perspective linking various scientific, social, and artistic fields; to nurture a holistic view of arts, sciences, humanities, and healing; and to publish and distribute literature on the relationship of mind, body, and nature.

> North Atlantic Books' publications are available through most bookstores. For further information, call 800-337-2665 or visit our website at www.northatlanticbooks.com. Substantial discounts on bulk quantities are available to corporations, professional associations, and other organizations. For details and discount information, contact our special sales department.

Library of Congress Cataloging-in-Publication Data

LaChance, Albert J.
  The modern Christian mystic : a unitive approach to the presence of God / Albert J. LaChance ; with a foreword by Carol Wallas LaChance ; a poem by Paul Weiss ; and an afterword by Sarah Robbins-Cole.
       p. cm.
  Includes bibliographical references and index.
  ISBN 978-1-55643-669-7 (pbk. : alk. paper)
  1. Mysticism. I. Title.
BV5082.3.L33 2007
248.2'2—dc22
                                        2007031415

1 2 3 4 5 6 7 8 9 VERSA 14 13 12 11 10 09 08 07

I'd like to dedicate this book to my first grandson C. Jonah Goodwin, born 6/30/07, and to all my grandchildren in the hope that my writings will support you in creating a future.
Your Papa and Gran have loved you since before you were conceived.

Contents

FOREWORD

By Carol Wallas LaChance

Many years ago, Albert and I used to offer Christian retreat weekends at various venues in New England. On a Friday afternoon we would pack up our station wagon with two young girls and all their toys, our wonderful babysitter Mary Grace, and a very energetic Springer spaniel. I remember one particular fall weekend, we were due to present to a group of Catholic nuns at a retreat house in Massachusetts. It had been a busy week and we all set off irritated and overwhelmed, trying to keep two young children, not to mention the dog, happy during the long car ride. Finally, we pulled into a beautiful tree-lined driveway with a gracious mansion at the end. As we parked, Albert and I got out and began to walk toward the rather imposing front door. He looked at me with something like panic spreading across his face. "What on earth are we going to do all weekend?" I grinned at him, knowing that even though we had done this before, we had not had adequate time to sit and prepare our talks and experiences. "We just have to love them," I said quietly. "That's all." As I remember it, the weekend was a great success. Our time with those lovely women was rich and nourishing. Of course, we received from them the love that we gave. They loved the fact that we were a traveling family, and that they could experience our lived spirituality as a couple and as parents. Once we began on Friday night with the first talk, everything just flowed from there.

I have often returned in my mind to those words of mine, said without conscious thought or reflection. It was as though they were spoken *in* me rather than *by* me. The power of them has informed my spiritual journey day by day. How can I allow the love of God to move through me to others and receive the love of God as it flows back to me? This movement of energy that I understand to be love is everywhere, vibrant in every tree as it sways in the breeze, present in my dog's adoring gaze as he stares at me, and available in every interaction in which I am truly present.

How simple and yet how difficult to make those words a reality day by day. Life has a way of complicating the flow of love throughout the universe, blocking and distorting it. All of us must surrender to reach what Eliot called this "condition of complete simplicity," where we live within the ballet of love. When I began my spiritual journey in earnest, I was a young woman. The experience that was the catalyst for so much change and growth for me was becoming a mother. To help me make sense of how to be and how to love, I looked for a spiritual guide and found mine in the person of Mary of Nazareth. Mary had not played a strong role in my religious upbringing but I loved her story and her bold prayer of surrender to God. I wondered about her life, I shared with her the mystery of carrying life, and I prayed to her to help me in my desire to surrender my life to God. I remember reading in Rosemary Haughton's book *The Passionate God,* her description of Mary as the "medium of exchange" between God and humanity. Ms. Haughton understood Mary's longing to love God to be so vulnerable, so total that God could take flesh in her womb. Mary offered herself body and soul and received body and soul, the Incarnation.

When our daughters were young, we played a game at night called "mad, sad, glad." The game involved my asking them what made them mad, then sad, then glad that day and then we talked about it. One night, when she was perhaps three years old, Becky lay in bed sucking her thumb, her Annie doll beside her, and I talked to her about Mary, the mother of Jesus, and how she had said "yes" to God. Becky looked at me sleepily, removed her thumb, and whispered "I'm like Mary, Mummy, I've said yes to being me." Those words, too, became a mantra on my journey. So many life experiences teach us to deny, reject, or abandon our true selves. Loving God fully must mean saying yes to becoming the person I was created to be, my essential self. It must mean allowing God's love to fill me, and then striving to love others from that fullness. As I write, Becky is carrying our first grandchild, a little boy. Watching her become a mother, become like Mary, become a co-creator with God of new life, is a wonderful gift. She continues to say yes to being who she is.

I have lived with Albert now for twenty-seven years and I have watched and shared his spiritual journey. His first creative work, when we were newly married, was a 1,400-line poetic cycle entitled "Jonah: A Prophecy at the Millennium." In one of the poems, he wrote about being "called to cleanse the windows to the sun" and I believe that this really is what his life has been about. His spiritual quest has always been a search to find a way to make God present to others, to find a way to give people a clear view of the Light, a true *experience* of God. He has suffered on his journey as he has struggled to cleanse the "windows" of his soul, and then share his experience with others. What I want to share with the reader in this foreword is that I have witnessed firsthand the integrity and the deep commitment Albert has brought to this search. His sincerity can be trusted. Trying to hang words on the deepest mystery of the universe is no simple task. We have had some great conversations over our favorite drink, English tea, as this book has been written. As always, I have been privileged to be part of Albert's wrestling match with truth. As anyone who has listened to him lecture, or sat with him as a client, or prayed with him knows, he is a wonderful human being. We continue to grope together toward a fuller expression of our essential selves.

In order to enter into the mystical Christianity that Albert has outlined here, I ask you to suspend judgment as far as that is possible and to allow the beauty of his vision and the love of God within it to embrace you. One of my spiritual guides on my journey once told me that the most important word in Christianity is *trust*. Without it we cannot allow God to love us, to change us, to mold us into the people He would have us be. Without trust we cannot say yes to life, we cannot surrender, and I am convinced that it is surrender that is the most vital aspect of our spiritual lives. My prayer is that you will allow the love that inspired this book to whisper its truth to you so that you can *experience* the mysticism of which Albert speaks. I know I can only do this when I open a place beneath my mind with all its judgments and commentaries, when I listen with my heart. Then, and only then, can I know the truth that while we are many, we all partake in The One who loves each of us eternally.

ACKNOWLEDGMENTS

I have been remiss in my first two books published by North Atlantic Books in not thanking my editor and, at this point, my friend Yvonne Cárdenas. Yvonne, you have been so cheerful, supportive, and patient throughout these three projects that I am shocked it has taken me this long. You are such a solid and pleasant person. Thank you. And, of course, my deepest thanks to Richard Grossinger and Lindy Hough, my publishers, without whose openness and support none of this would be taking place.

To my daughter Becky, who is my own first-born, my colleague and helper—and who, together with my son-in-law Chuck, has blessed my life with my grandson. You have helped me since day one with this book and have contributed so very much to it. Thank you.

To my other daughter Kateri, whose passion and humor continue to engulf me in their flames. Your career and life open before you and so many will find healing and love through your heart. You have enriched my life—and, oh yes, I'm pulling for Ian. I love you.

To my life-friend and love Carol, who breathes life into all my days and all my work. Who knows what is mine and what is yours at this point? This book, like our family, is best described as ours. Thank you and I love you.

To Thomas Berry, who shaped my worldview and who has modeled greatness at every stage along the way.

To the real brothers of my heart—Remi, PK, and Paul—and their wives Mary, Ana, and Alex. It has been said that if you have one real friend in life, you're a rich man. Already, I have had three lifetimes' worth.

To Adrian and Sarah Robbins-Cole, whose lovely little family boasts of two priests, a knight, and a damsel. I love you all. And to all members of All Saints in Peterborough, New Hampshire, every one, you have been the unexpected and deeply appreciated nest for my soul. Thank you.

To old friends like Cindy Acorace and to my newest friends Catherine Martin and Matthew Taylor and the little sangha we've become.

For my deceased friends Jimmy Preston and my young love, Rebecca Smith. I have gone on loving you both and am eager to meet you one day on the other side.

To those friends presently estranged—James Aponovich, Brian Swimme, Angela Manno, Kathleen Harrity, Lois Cote, and Stan Fortuna. I go on loving you in absentia.

And always, always, always my English family and their spouses. My life and work has been made possible by you and no dedication can capture my appreciation. Nonetheless, thank you.

To all of you who have given kindness and care to the pain and stress I carry in my body—the chiropractors, the massage therapists, and others. My ability to live and move have so often been dependent on your kindness and generosity. This is also true at the level of healing that you have given me regarding the treatment of my body in my childhood and in the addiction illness of my twenties. Thank you all, deeply.

Last, I want to thank Billy Brown, who met me in the desert of my anguish following the breaking of the news by the *Boston Globe* regarding the crimes against children in New England. You met me in the center of a shattered life when I did not even know that you were in the midst of an even more devastating walk yourself. You make Christ real for me and support my transcendence into the Christ-mind that made this book possible. Thanks, Billy.

A Note to the Reader

The word *poet* comes from the Greek word *poieo,* which is the verb "to make." Thus, a poet is a wordmaker and I've made some words in this book. I want to explain their meanings and my purpose in making them.

First, *ChristLogos*—as one word. The Greek word *Christus* means "anointed" and *Logos* means "divine revelation of God through Christ." So, ChristLogos means "the anointed revelation of God through Christ." Too much emphasis on the person of Jesus, especially because of the Pauline literature, has, in my opinion, diminished the mystical importance of the Logos as God's revelation through the created order. So I am attempting to reassert the mysticism by the creation of this word uniting the two.

Next, in writing about sexual union, I have avoided typical usages such as gay, heterosexual, homosexual, and others. The word *gay* is defined in Webster's dictionary as "in or showing a joyous, merry mood; cheerfully lively; given to or abounding in social or other pleasures; as 'a gay social event.' Given over to frivolous pleasure; dissipated, licentious. Bright or brilliantly colored; showily adorned." Thus the word gay can be used to describe anyone who expresses gaity. Webster's final definition listed as "slang" is homosexual. So, disliking all the words available to talk about the issues of one-sex union and heterosexual union, I chose to create my own:

Samesex: The word is clear and simple and lacks all the inflammatory connotations of many other legitimate as well as cruel appellations.

Bothsex: Again, plainly accurate, male and female present (and which could be expressed as *fe/male*). In neither case is there any positive or negative loading of the word.

I hope these words gain currency.

INTRODUCTION

This book is about God.

However, this book is not meant to be theology and I don't even claim it to be "the Truth." It is, however, my truth. While trained in theology, I write from experience and not from dogma. It is my attempt to share what I have learned and experienced over the last four decades and hope that perhaps you will find something of value here. This book is about mysticism.

Mysticism is experiential. As such, it is not derived. Dogma comes from reflection upon experience, one's own or another's. Thus it is derived. Please do not take me for an anti-dogmatist because I've said that. Dogma is the codified understanding drawn from experiential truth. It is helpful, and even necessary. However, it will not be the focus of this book.

If you are a Christian, of whatever denomination, you can agree with other Christians, of whatever denomination, on at least two things. The first is that Jesus Christ was a divine person. The second is that he was also a human person. On these two things, the three major vehicles of Christianity agree, whether Catholic, Orthodox, mainline Protestant, or Evangelical. Whatever else Christians believe or know about God, these two fundamentals can be agreed upon. Thus for all Christians, God is a being with whom they can have a personal relationship, and in Jesus Christ God became a human person.

While neither Jews nor Muslims believe that Jesus Christ was divine, they both agree that he was a human person. And they both agree that God is a divine being experienced as either Yahweh or

Allah. So, all Jews, Christians, and Muslims experience God as a being with whom they can have a personal relationship. God, then, if you are Jew, Christian, or Muslim, is always a divine being and not something or some state of consciousness.

Many native or indigenous forms of religion also relate to the presence of a divine being. Many, if not most, forms of Hinduism are devotional in the same way. Many other Eastern religions conceive of God as a divine being as well. There are those in the West, who, after some experience of Buddhism and other nondevotional religions, view "God as divine being" religions as somehow naive. I am someone who, after more than thirty years of deep and respectful study of Buddhism and other Eastern systems, goes on *experiencing* God as a divine being who personally relates to me. You'll notice that throughout this book I have actually framed Christian mysticism in a Buddhist fashion. You would have to look long and hard to find a non-Buddhist who holds Buddhism in higher esteem than I do. Nonetheless, I am God-centered or theocentric, Christ-centered or christocentric, and personalist or one who believes in the personal nature of God.

Before the first half of the first millennium of Christianity was over, Christianity was rejuvenated by the ideas of the Greek philosopher Plato, through the contribution of St. Augustine of Hippo. Early in the second millennium the same thing happened again, this time through Thomas Aquinas as he incorporated the philosophy of Aristotle into Christianity. I have sincerely come to believe that if Christian mysticism, the flower of Christian practice and experience, is to revitalize Western culture and all of culture generally, then it must pass through the lens of Buddhism. The pristine clarity of the Buddhist-Taoist lens, when used to reexamine Christian dogma, can breathe new spiritual life into that dogma without violence to the dogmatic truths themselves. But I digress—that will become more evident as we go on. I note it in passing in order to "own" the Buddhist influence you may sense throughout this book. I'll also "own" that I am a practicing Episcopal-Catholic mystic. Some history follows on how I came to the unitive understanding that led to this book.

From My Awful Place

There is a place in the deepest parts of my memory that I call "my awful place." I don't want to compare my suffering to, for instance, Holocaust survivors, for that would make trivial the cosmic proportions of their suffering. On the other hand, I don't want to fall prey to the trap of many survivors of family and cultural violence in the form of thinking "I'm just making a fuss," or "It couldn't really have been that bad." It was terrible and there has been, and at certain times still is, terrible suffering emanating from my awful place.

The Family

My mother put the lie to the notion that all perpetrators of domestic violence are "he," and all victims "her." My mother was a *ferocious* pre-Vatican II Catholic who herself had grown up in a violent household, and in the cultural expression of French Canadian Catholicism. I loved my mother, but she was nonetheless given to long moments of utter madness. She often beat me breathless for trivial reasons and even for no apparent reason at all. She beat me awake in the morning from a deep sleep. The blows to my face seemed at first to be part of my dreaming. The awakening was to a nightmare. At sixty years old, I still find it hard for my wife to move through the bedroom in the night without a massive startle response and greatly increased heart rate.

Without going too deeply into the details, my mother's violence in the family was supported by a spiritual pathology present in the Catholic Church at that time. Even outside my home, school offered no safe haven, for here too I was beaten by brothers and priests who taught in my Catholic schools. In many ways, my abuse was so fundamentally damaging due to its connection in my mind with God. Expressed in both my French Canadian home and grammar school, the Church had been overrun by what I like to call a spiritual totalitarianism. Like its political counterpart, my experience of Catholicism was one of fear and powerlessness. I felt trapped, relying completely on the mercy of the brothers and priests who beat me. How can a child learn to find comfort in God when he feels that God himself is beating him, humiliating him, punishing him for being bad? How can a child learn to pray when he is ridiculed for reciting a prayer incorrectly? To this day, I am not sure if anyone can fully recover from this type of abuse, an abuse of the soul. It is my belief that the epidemic of personality disorders in today's age can be seen as a logical consequence of the violation of the soul that many in my generation and subsequent generations have suffered.

The Second Vatican Council attempted to reverse some of these rampant violations, to open the door to change and reform. The energy of Vatican II and its progressive doctrines of equality, human dignity, and empowerment to the laity of the Church radiated throughout the world. However, even to this day, anything even resembling the full vision of Vatican II has never been truly implemented in Church practice, and many others such as myself would continue to suffer due to the violations by Catholic religious.

That spiritual totalitarianism was founded upon a rigid and frigid understanding of the pope as the earthly representative or even incarnation of Christ, with a succession of ironclad hierarchical offices. Most frequently in my experience then and now, these offices are occupied by people who really require the structures in order to have a sense of self. The priests and brothers who occupied the schools in which I was taught were frequently, as I look back now, deeply dissociated and developmentally arrested men who were really boy-men, both emotionally and sexually, and certainly spiritually. The events recently disclosed by the *Boston Globe* that led to the exposing of what has been called the "greatest crime against children in the history of

New England" all took place during my childhood and some of these events were perpetrated directly upon my own person. It is from that kind of totalitarianism that so many people from my generation have run headlong from Christianity, thinking that what they were taught was Christianity. That was *not* Christianity.

Returning to the question of the Second Vatican Council, my own thinking leads me to the following. The Church cannot have it both ways: the councils and the documents that result from them, in this case, the documents of Vatican II, cannot both be inspired by the Holy Spirit, which they claim, and at the same time not be implemented. If the experiential truth of the breath of the Holy Spirit is breathed through the council, then that experiential truth must be God's will for the operation of the Church. To not implement the will of God is to then produce a second collective heresy. One could say that to impede that voice is to commit sin against the Holy Spirit, warned of in the Gospel according to John.

I was an adolescent in the sixties, a time of incredible turmoil. Luckily for me, in 1960 John F. Kennedy became the youngest U.S. president. Here was a different kind of Catholic in a very prominent position. As a teenager, I'd forego *American Bandstand* for a Kennedy news conference. My need to have a model of something other than the degradation and lack of dignity of my own experience was fulfilled by John F. Kennedy. In the time of "Camelot" there was another sense of what it meant to be Catholic. On the inside, Jack and Jackie became my idealized parents. I had begun to peer out of my awful place. My psychological and spiritual life was rescued to the extent that I was able to project it upon John F. Kennedy and Jacqueline Kennedy and, later, Robert F. Kennedy. I began to look to great ideas and vision, a tangible vision that I experienced from them. I owe them a huge debt of gratitude. But in 1963, at age sixteen, I was sitting in cafeteria study hall next to Karen and Marilyn when the news came over the loudspeaker, "The president of the United States has been shot and is dead. Let us pray."

In my personal life there were friends. I fell in love at seventeen with a girl I dated for three years. My sisters left home. I graduated high school in 1965, 409th in my class of 563. I was angry and shut down. My chosen father, John F. Kennedy, was dead. My real father told me I was a bum and a loser—his own projection onto me, I can see now. Vietnam was heating up. At the edge of my awareness I could still hear the vision in Martin Luther King, Jr. and Bobby Kennedy. I was listening to Beatles' love songs while holding and kissing my girlfriend—but, in my awful place I began to hear only the Rolling Stones: "I was schooled with a strap right across my back."

Soon Martin Luther King, Jr. and Bobby Kennedy would be dead. The leadership of the baby boomers would pass from the Kennedys and King to McCartney and Lennon, Morrison, Hendrix, and Joplin. My girlfriend would leave me. The idealism would slowly die. The addictive dimension of the hippie movement would become the whole movement. The whole country seemed to move to my awful place. I staggered through my twenties, drunk, stoned, tripping, and dying one day at a time. I called myself an atheist, though I was not. I pretended to be a hippie, though I was not. Everything that I was then was something that I was not. I was totally lost and profoundly unhappy. What kept me alive was the memory of love. I had felt genuine love, I knew it existed and could not un-know that knowledge. I was in hell but I remembered better times.

It is hard to understand now in a culture riddled with epidemic addiction that the initial search in LSD was the search for a mystical experience in a culture arthritic with spiritual totalitarianism. It began as a struggle to "break on through to the other side." Instead of freedom, the end result has been cultural pathology, environmental pathology, and spiritual bipolarity. On the one side there is a right-wing neoconservative dogmatism. On the other, a left-wing fundamentalism expressed in the erosion of moral norms that have guided this culture and all other cultures for millennia, and the attempt to make normative that which has always been viewed as morally detrimental. This bipolarity between right and left continues to ravage the culture, while most people who think about and discuss it find themselves to be more readily described as centrists. The growing numbers of independents among voting registrations are an indication of this disenchantment with the collective bipolar disorder we all struggle with.

In 1970, I asked God to make me a poet. I'd half-decided that I *was* one the year before while reading Walt Whitman and saying to myself, "Hell, I can do this." I did not say that in 1972 when I came across T. S. Eliot's *Four Quartets*. I had been reading lots of poetry between 1969 and 1972, but nothing prepared me for this! *Four Quartets* completely changed my life.

Eliot would be my next father. I devoured biographies about him and began to memorize large tracts of *Four Quartets*. I read that he had studied Sanskrit at Harvard and that he was deeply involved in Buddhism. Later he decided that Western humans must find meaning and practice of mysticism in Western religion, in Western mysticism. He left for England and became an Anglican mystic.

There was a group of people missionizing in New Hampshire at the time called "The Holy Order of Mans." I studied and prayed with them. They had a communion rite and a baptism rite, and I was reintroduced to sacramental religion. They and I were also studying Buddhism. Before long, with Eliot's ideas giving me permission, I returned to the Eucharist in the Roman Catholic Church. I continued studying Huang Po, Hui Hai, Christmas Humphries, Edward Conze, Joseph Campbell, Erich Neumann, and so very many others. One night in the mid-1970s, I had a peculiar experience due to some of this studying, namely, a small book by Pierre Teilhard de Chardin called *How I Believe*. As my insomnia kept me awake, I suddenly had a vision of The One in its evolutionary dynamic. I literally experienced all of existence as one fabric, and myself totally indistinguishable from any other part. This experience in some ways represented a turning point, a moment where a synthesis began to form between all of my studies—science, cosmology, mythology, West and East, sacramental, and experiential. That synthesis would be the earliest expression of what now has become this book. Buddhism for a path, Eucharist for food, but still something was missing. What?

On December 4, 1978, I woke after a weekend of drinking and knew I could no longer live with my internal pain. I called out to God for help and, thanks to God, I have not had a mind-altering substance to this day. I couldn't do it alone. So, in delirium tremens and not knowing it, I began attending AA meetings. I discovered AA's twelve steps and, in doing so, a whole new understanding of the Catholic sacrament of reconciliation. Confession was the missing piece. Buddhism, Eucharist, and confession. I'd found the way out of my awful place.

I met Carol in 1979 in a course I was teaching on poetry. We married in 1980. In 1981 Becky was born and in 1986 Kateri. Between those signal events in my life, Carol and I explored Catholic sacramental marriage while I studied theology and she behavioral science. We both finished in 1983 and went off to Oakland, California, so that I could do a master's degree under Matthew Fox at Holy Names College. Carol and I had already read the three books he had out at that time, but it was his book *Compassion* that really shook me. I'd always loved the planet in the form of my beloved New Hampshire and had also begun to think about the cosmos and physics in its mystical phase. In *Compassion* it all came together—Catholicism, Buddhism, AA, C. G. Jung, ecology, and cosmology. So off to California!

In my mind Matthew Fox deserves a great deal of credit for his work. While I was studying with him, I met Brian Swimme, a gravitational physicist, and his teacher, Thomas Berry. My study of Teilhard de Chardin had prepared me for Berry's cutting-edge thinking and his "New Story," which would change my life and thinking forever. When I left California in 1984 I went home to study with Thomas Berry one-on-one for five years at his Riverdale Center for Religious Research. The study of the Tao Te Ching prepared me for the voice of Thomas Berry, who was not only founding president of the

American Teilhard Association, but also was working in the Asian Institute at St. John's University while emerging documents from the East were being translated for the Western world. Having met Thomas Berry on February 8, 1984, my father's birthday, I suddenly was granted a unitive glimpse of the universe-Earth-life process as one. In Thomas Berry I found a fulfillment of what was then, already, a decade and a half of searching. Thomas Berry's work is as much responsible for this book as my own.

From 1985 to 1989 I went to Riverdale, New York for a weekend three times yearly. Together Tom and I covered all of his Twelve Principles for Understanding the Universe and the Role of the Human in the Universe Process. Each principle was framed as a one-semester course. He'd suggest anywhere from five to twelve books on a principle and I'd go back to New Hampshire and read. When I returned to Riverdale we'd discuss that principle and go on to the next. During that time, and at Brian's and his suggestion, I wrote *Greenspirit,* my first book.

Now it was the mid-90s. I began PhD work at the Union Institute, which would take seven years and nearly kill me. It threatened my marriage and, actually and in truth, my sanity. But in that time, I created from all my prior experience and, adding the colossal insight of Ken Wilbur, a new synthesis called the "architecture of the soul," which will soon be followed by a new therapy to go with that model.

I am still a practicing Christian mystic, now in the Anglican denomination. I'm still studying Buddhism and all the other topics mentioned herein. My awful place? From the violent and abusive family of origin I've built a twenty-seven-year marriage with two beautiful daughters that anyone would brag about. Carol, while never addicted to alcohol, and I choose to be sober, me since 1978, she since August 1980. Neither of my daughters have "experimented" with drugs or alcohol to this day. One is twenty-six and one is twenty-two at the time of this writing. From the abusive and dysfunctional experience of school, I've become a Doctor of Integral Psychology, have had a healing practice for seventeen years, and have taught in two colleges and a university. I have a unique and powerful experience of the personhood of Jesus Christ. And Mr. Eliot? I have produced a long mystical poem called *Jonah,* my attempt to put my journey into words, while understanding that there are those "whom one cannot hope to emulate." My journey has been an experience of the grace of God. The writing of this book represents the presentation of this whole journey.

My main motivation in writing this book is to offer to young people an opportunity to bring forth their best in a practice of Christian faith that is believable, ecological, mystical, cosmological, truly Christian, and meditative. I invite readers, both young and old, to enter into this book as a simple way in which to reexamine their whole understanding of what it means to be Christian. My long-term hope with this, as with all my books, is to provide some form of healing to the pain-filled culture in which we live, as well as to the pain-filled life community in which it is embedded. This is my life and this my prayer: that each of you can find in some way a small experience this very day of Christ's healing touch. In that experience perhaps we can then turn to each other, heal one another, heal the tension between human cultures, and heal the terrible plight of the Earth as she suffers under the weight of a deluded and addicted culture. Our one hope, it seems to me, is a practice that comes from Buddhism with a focus that is Christian.

In order for us to move forward as a culture, we must begin to seek out common ground, a common language through which we can identify with one another across the religious lines. Mysticism offers such a tool because it seeks experience, not theology. God is God in every tradition. In a world such as ours that uses violence in the name of God to torture, terrorize, and kill, clearly theology is no longer working. We must begin to focus on what unites us rather than what divides us as citizens of the Earth. If Christianity wishes to be part of the solution, we must recreate ourselves. We must convert Christianity.

PART I

The Unitive Vision

A Note on the Word *Unitive*

My recent book *The Architecture of the Soul: A Unitive Model of the Human Person* (North Atlantic Books, 2005) was originally titled *Integral Psychology*. It was based upon my doctoral thesis and in it I described myself as an "integralist." At that time, I thought I had named a whole new psychology until just weeks before completing my thesis, when Ken Wilber came out with a book called *Integral Psychology*! I had come to the title by extensive reading of his and, later, Sri Aurobindo's work. So I changed my thesis title to "The Architecture of the Soul: An Integral Model of the Human Person." Thus is titled the doctoral thesis at the Union Institute where I became, I think, the first credentialed integral psychologist in the year 2000. When the thesis was shortened and became a trade book, I changed the subtitle to "A *Unitive* Model of the Human Person." So, in my mind, *unitive* and *integral* are nearly synonymous. That is not, of course, to say that Albert LaChance and Ken Wilber are synonymous! Still, our work has significant overlaps and, to be sure, I am in his debt. Ken and I met for a whole brilliant morning in Denver, Colorado to discuss both the similarities and the differences in our work.

It is nothing new for Christian theologians to indicate that for a Christian understanding of the spirit of God to be true or complete, that understanding must address both the immanence as well as the transcendence of God's being. Thus, transcendence (the outside, the whole, the greater-than the whole) plus immanence (the inside, the internal, the subset) together equals the truth of God's "unitive" being. In a similar way, Eastern plus Western equals unitive, tradition plus experience equals unitive, soul plus body equals unitive, life plus death, man plus woman, spirit plus matter all equal unitive. Unitive, then, equals the recognition that when God created the universe, there was nothing *(ex nihilo)* to fashion it of but the divine presence itself! For the mystic, then, despite frequent appearances to the contrary, the whole is divine and remains divine and whole in each of its parts. This is why evil always gives way to good, to truth, to its original, essential, and core being. The unitive presence of God is the only ultimate fact! It is the source, the creation, and when truly felt or experienced, it creates the wholeness it signifies. Unitive includes the pre-existent creator, and the creator's presence in the *now* of creation. Mysticism in all wisdom traditions, whether Eastern, Western, indigenous, scientific, or spiritual, is an experiential search for The One who makes unitive the many or the all. This book presents third-millennium Christianity in that unitive light, a modern Christian mysticism.

CHAPTER I

The Silence of God

It can be heard in the context of traditional Christian theology that there is an ontological (*ontos* is Greek for "being") chasm between the human and the divine. Frequently, it is further held that Jesus bridged this ontological chasm, bringing the hand of God as it were and the hand of the human together. This has always struck me as a peculiar position to hold when viewed through the mystical lens. While the mystical lens would certainly support the transcendence of God in the sense that God is more than the sum of all of creation, there would be no breach in the being of God and the being of creation, the latter flowing directly from the former as an extension and expression of itself.

Nonetheless, one can certainly understand without the mystical lens how such a position would be held, especially in defending Christian doctrine from misunderstandings derived from pantheists. In any case, a more adequate reconciliation for the Christian mystic would be that there is prior to what scientists call the event horizon, a vast and infinite silence out of which the universe is made manifest. That silence could be called the outer edge of the pre-temporal, pre-spatial presence of God. In Hinduism, the term *sachidananda* describes that infinite silence from which the universe by extension derives its being. Beyond the silence, in the direction of infinity, the essence and being of God may from time to time be experienced in moments of profound meditative elation. We could almost think of God as an infinite spiral galaxy, the outer band of which is the universe. The space between the outer band and the next band is the great silence and the being of God "thickening" as we journey from band to silence to band to silence toward the center, which is unspeakable light. The foregoing was of course merely a metaphor, an attempt to reduce to language my own experience of God in meditation.

This experience of The One crosses all barriers of tradition in describing "that ultimate mystery whence all *things* emerge into being." It is not as though there was a different kind or dimension of God preceding the Trinity, but more that in a direct approach to the presence of God all concepts, including the Trinity, melt before the radiance, the brilliance, the unspeakable "heat" of God's being. All symbols derive from the silence that extends beyond the event horizon of space/time and energy/matter. The unitive vision, however, makes it experientially clear that the present moment in which I write this and the present moment in which you read this are equally extensions of space/time and energy/matter, themselves extensions of the silence, itself an extension of the being of God.

So, in the following chapter, we will talk about the doctrine of the Trinity as it tumbled out of the ChristLogos, the universe, the silence, and the being of God.

CHAPTER 2

Christ and the Trinity

Some physicists are quick to warn us that for physicists there is no such thing as "before space," "before time," "before energy," "before matter," or "before the beginning." Humans are products of space/time, of energy/matter; how can they speak of a "before" that does not include them? To do so, humans would have to be "outside" the universe and there is no "outside"! It is true that humans are manifestations of a temporal/spatial universe. We think, feel, and possess instincts, all functions of a material brain that is conceived, lives, and dies. Thought is the "voice" of our cognitive brain or neocortex; we secrete thoughts. Affect, or emotion, is the "voice" of our mammalian inner brain or limbic system; we secrete feelings. Instinct is the "voice" of our reptilian brain or brain stem; we secrete intuition. All of these, it is true, are subject to conception and death, space and time, energy and matter. But, what if we also had a fourth voice?

What if we are not completely determined by space/time? By energy/matter? What if our knowing had a fourth voice, not limited by the laws of physics? Einstein seemed to be pointing to this in his book *Out of My Later Years*. In it, he reported that not only did he see no conflict between science and spirituality (except for those who don't know any better!), but he described his own theories as products of spiritual experiences! Our mythologies and cosmogonies globally attest to the sensing of an Ultimate Mystery preceding and/or transcending time and space and the source of time, space, energy, and matter. Most people sense the truth of this in a visceral, a felt,

5

way; we sense that *existence* precedes *existents.* The universe expresses intentionality and is deliberate. We try to capture this sensing in stories of how someone or something did the creating. We sense that we are more than what we can know, that we know more than we can prove. The universality of this fourth kind of knowing is itself a form of proof, of repeatability.

The Christian understanding of this Ultimate Mystery is expressed as the doctrine of the Trinity. It is held that God, one in three, is, always has been, and always will be. This makes sense when God as one is understood as being itself, consciousness itself. Time, space, energy, and matter are extensions, or emergent expressions of the Divine Being itself. Before any manifest *beings* there was already the Being of the Father. Through the ChristLogos the universe was made manifest. This ChristLogos would later become incarnate as Jesus of Nazareth. The Holy Spirit is the trembling presence of God throughout creation. Father (the unmanifest), Son (the manifest), Holy Spirit (the divine presence)—three persons, one God. We can know something about this mystery through thought. We can feel something about the wonder of it through affect. We can intuit truth, reality, bio-signaling, through instinct. But to *experience* the mystery of our own being we must awaken, clarify, and listen through the fourth voice. We do this through meditation and the spectacular gift of the Eucharist. We do this by practicing Christian mysticism.

This is the meaning of *imago dei,* the image of God. We too are three—thought, feeling and instinct; and in the fourth voice, we are one. We can know something of someone prior to meeting that person. This knowledge, the ideas, might create feelings in us about people even before we meet them. Deeper than thoughts or feelings, however, we might have intuitions about them, born of our instinctual responses. But only by our experience of knowing people can we have the ability to truly speak of loving them. With some people, there is always more to discover, more to know, more to love. Discovery emerges directly from our experience of them. Mysticism is the knowing of God gained from personal experience. Christian mysticism is the knowing of God through Christ. Our love for God, God's love for us, *IS* the Holy Spirit! The mind of the fourth voice *IS* The One! Scripture, ideas, and dogma can and do point toward the experience. But only mysticism and its practice can illuminate scripture, ideas, and dogma into the experience of God.

To return to Trinity: God does not have three "pieces" or "parts." God is one expressed as many. The three persons are best understood as three dynamics of The One, of the whole being of God. We often experience ourselves in a similar way. We might even say, "I'm one person on the job, another with my family, and still another in the woods with my dog." We are speaking of three dynamics of the one person each of us is. As mentioned, we can think of the Father as the unmanifest mystery out of which the Son/Logos is made manifest and within which the Holy Spirit is felt to be present. So, to be "moved by the Spirit" is to experience the vital flow of God's presence deep within our being, or more accurately *as* our being. For Christians, Jesus is the full depth of divine mystery made manifest in human flesh. For many, Jesus the human being represents the most accessible, the most approachable, image of God. Jesus is the incarnation (en-flesh-ment) of the mercy and creativity of God. His oneness with the mysterious depth of the Father and Spirit is clearly expressed in the Gospel according to John 14:8–10:

> Philip said, "Lord, show us the Father and then
> we shall be satisfied." Jesus said to him, "Have I been
> with you all this time, Philip, and you still do not
> know me? Anyone who has seen me has seen the
> Father, so how can you say, 'Show us the Father?'
> Do you now believe that I am in the Father and the
> Father is in me?"

The following thought experiment might help. Imagine for a moment that you have never lived on Earth. Perhaps you are a visitor from a distant galaxy who has never experienced the blue water-planet. Upon your arrival here, you are shown for the very first time a beaker of water, a chunk of ice, and a glass cylinder of steam. Imagine your disbelief when told that they are all H_2O in three different states. Your own sense would protest! One is a liquid, one a cold rock, and one a hot gas! They seem to be separate and distinct, and yet three states of one thing, H_2O. The complete phenomenon of H_2O is never separate in any of those three states. Likewise for the Christian, the one God is manifest in three persons, complete and undivided. God has infinite mysterious depth, which precedes space/time and energy/matter. The very being of God is made manifest as cosmos. God, as the Being, is incarnate in all flesh. Mysticism is the experience of our own being as an expression of that oneness, to become aware of ourselves as that oneness. To experience our own awareness is to become aware of God. To be aware of our own presence is to experience the presence of God as Holy Spirit.

The one precedes the many as the unmanifest precedes the manifest. A taproot of the great cosmos tree is the Trinity itself made manifest by The One. Evolution—cosmic, geological, biological, or cultural—is the dynamic through which the many grow from the one. Once again, the eternal unmanifest can be called Father. The manifest cosmos can be called Son. The sentience inherent in all creation can be called the Spirit. Jesus of Nazareth was The One in flesh who was crucified and rose from the dead. The Son was the appearance of God in creation, a creature of himself! Like Jesus, we are to be leaves of the great cosmic tree, or branches of the vine. In John 15:5, Jesus makes this clear by saying, "I am the vine, you are the branches. Whoever remains in me with me in him bears fruit in plenty, for cut off from me you can do nothing." Our common trunk is the whole of evolution and our roots reach back to the Trinity itself. The deepest memory we bear within is the memory of paradise, or eternity. To remember that memory is to transcend space/time, energy/matter, and the event horizon of physics. To remember is to reclaim our source. To remember is to regain Paradise. We may never measure that memory with mathematics, but we can know it! In meditation we come to know through the fourth voice of our being.

CHAPTER 3

The Cosmos: The Sacrament of God

Imagine light, the first light, the light of God streaming over the horizon of the beginning. Thus was the universe conceived of nothing but the ChristLogos of God. In that sense, the universe is itself a virgin birth, born of no-thing but the consciousness of God. The universe is a divine child born of the selfhood of God expressed as light. Imagine for a moment a gushing font of fire spraying forth into the dark womb of nothingness. Each of us is a recent expression of the same divine universe, and what we imagine to be the beginning is, in fact, our memory of the beginning! What began as the pure consciousness of God became at first the radiation phase of the early universe. When that radiation cooled, it became matter; consciousness is $E = mc^2$! The "stuff" of God's consciousness is the light, life, and matter that are this cosmos. The apostle John had this experiential knowledge in mind when he wrote the prologue to his Gospel:

> In the beginning was the Word, and the Word was
>   with God
> and the Word was God.
> He was with God in the beginning.
> Through him all things came into being,
> and not one thing came into being except through
>   him.
> What has come into being in him was life,
> and life that was the light of all people.

The light shines in darkness,
and darkness could not overpower it.

JOHN 1:1–5

The creative consciousness of God is called Logos or Word. Jesus of Nazareth was and is the incarnation of that consciousness; so is the universe, and so are we!

As this burst of Logos/Light began to "freeze out" into matter, the first helium and hydrogen were born. Hydrogen would later combine with oxygen to form Earth's water—water for oceans, the Jordan, the Ganges, baptism. The word *cosmos* means order and the universe possessed an inherent *Logic* (*Log*-os), or law. This law is an expression of the consciousness of God within energy/matter. Gravity, electromagnetism, the strong and weak nuclear forces provide the universe with the ability to self-structure. For the Christian mystic, that self-structuring is a function of the mind of ChristLogos. Law presumes intelligence. The presence of intelligence presumes will or design. The creation and organization of space/time and energy/matter presume a creator. The Judeo-Christian "memory" of that creation is recorded in Genesis 1:1–31. This event is our own deepest memory. God is not speaking "into" matter, but from within matter. With the exception of verses 14–19, the sequence is roughly the same as the story of evolution: "In the beginning, ... evening came and morning came, the sixth day."

Stars formed, evolved, burned out, and swelled into novas, exploded, and rose again as second-generation stars. Our own sun is a a second generation, a reborn star. The planets revolving around it were parts of its rebirth from a single proto-solar disk. The incarnate creativity of God walked one day on the third planet out from the star, the blue water-planet, Earth. Steam rising from the hot planet cooled into water. Seas formed and soils formed and life emerged. In the midst of a profusion of life forms, wheat and grape emerged. Wheat and grape would in time become the ritual meal we call the Eucharist.

The same law and ordering expressed by God as self-making, self-governance at the universal and planetary levels also appeared in the life community. The seasons, the cycles of water, of weather, of rock and the layering of soils, the life forms of the seas and the land, the experience of themselves and their means of interaction—these and more are all expressions of the inherent ChristLogos. What we call "ecology" is the presence of God in matter expressed as law, order, and governance. Territoriality, migration routes, the courses of rivers and air streams, the tides—these and more are all ultimately governed by the four fundamental forces, and are all expressions of the mind of God, the Almighty, maker of Heaven and Earth. Pollution of air and water, destruction of forests and soils and species, and all the eco-crimes are the refusal on our part to allow God's will to be done on Earth as it is in Heaven. Christian mysticism is a yielding of our wills to the will of the Spirit, of the ChristLogos. All else is an affront to The One through whom all things came into being. Our refusal often leads to the addictive lure of false gods. More on that later.

In the same way that the whole divine self is fully present in each person of the Trinity, the whole divine self is present in every star, every planet, and every moon. The whole divine self meets us in every wind, every drop of water, every handful of soil. The whole divine self is present to us in our own interior experience of mind, of emotion, of intuition. The whole divine self meets us in every animal, every person, every culture. The whole divine self meets us in every cell, atom, particle, and quantum. All things, all beings, are at the same time uniquely themselves, trembling with sentience and, at the same time, caught up in The One who is God. We are inseparable from the whole because we are an expression of the whole. We are part of a cosmos that was, is, and will be the sacrament of God, the unitive presence of God. We are inseparable from The One because we are made of The One!

Before space and time, before energy and matter, there was only the eternal Being, the unmanifest One, God. Unitive experience of our own interior "self-sense" awakens our souls to allow the beauty and truth to shine forth from within. When the soul is alive to shine outward to others, when we "let our light shine to all," we are unitive with the Now, and the Now is where God is evolving from within us. A culture of such people can create that "city on a hill." Truth and justice are unitive experiences within which are framed our laws on the "outside." Unitive experience, Christian mysticism, creates "a way, a truth, and a life," to humans and nonhumans alike. The darkness of lies, heresies (half-truths), and false selves cannot darken that light because they cannot comprehend that light!

We may not always be aware that we are the presence of God in this present form, in this time, this place. However, at moments of ecstasy, whether from joy or from pain, we open, we awaken, and we know. In those moments, we experience ourselves as local venues of the nonlocal, universal presence of God's being. God's presence is the spirit of Christ in us. From time to time, *if we practice* the Eucharist and meditation, the white-hot fire of that presence erupts in us and floods our consciousness. At those moments we experientially remember our oneness with the whole. This same experience happens when we truly fall in love—a mutual opening, a mutual awakening, a mutual knowing. In true Eucharistic experience, we lose the constricted being of the ego-self and become more and more the universal self in this present form. Our interior sentience or sensitivity awakens, lights up, and we become aware that we are The One in this present form. We then become community through communion with The One in others, each of whom are The One in present form. In true worship, the exultation causing us to praise God *IS* God! The urge to pray, the experience of prayer, and the object of prayer are all God, Alpha, NOW, and Omega! My term for this is "devotional nonduality." Mysticism is the worship of God as we experience our oneness with God. The eternal Father made manifest in his son, experienced as spirit within us, is the kingdom "in our midst."

From the fire of Genesis to the heat in our own bodies, from the food on our tables and altars, the four great laws have sculpted our reality for us all. The animals, plants, and insects, rocks and rivers, soils and storms are all inherently governed by gravity, electromagnetism, and the two nuclear forces. These laws are the outlines of God's thought in matter, the way in which God thinks a universe into being and sustains it. Behind them all, manifesting and uniting them, is The One, the spirit who is God. Each existent is like a small god, trillions of little gods united in the one spirit of God. In this sense, polytheism is just another version of monotheism, monotheism being a subsequent realization to the former. St. John was hinting at this in John 10:30. In speaking to them, Jesus said, "I and the Father are one."

The universe exhibits the law and ordering of the mind of its creator. Every manifestation of God exhibits the uniqueness, sentience, and oneness that *IS* God! Every existent is a manifestation of the pre-existence and present existence of God. Jesus of Nazareth is a manifestation of the pre-existent Father and present existence of the Spirit; they are all the One. The universe is a community of existents, comprising one *uni*-verse. We are surrounded by *gods,* are *gods*—and there is only one *God.*

CHAPTER 4

Earth: The Sacrament of the Cosmos

The torn and tortured body writhing on the cross at Calvary was that of a specific man, Jesus. It was, like our own bodies, composed of soil from food, from water and air and sunlight. We are told that it suffered, died, and was buried. We are also told that three days later it would breathe again, walk again, eat and drink again; it lived again! From Friday afternoon until Sunday morning it remained in an earthen cave, womb of the Resurrection. During that time, we are told, Jesus "descended among the dead" before rising again. We saw in the previous chapter that the cosmos was and is an expansion of the unmanifest into the manifest mystery of God. Planet Earth emerged in the cosmos along with the sun and other planets ten billion years following that initial expansion into time and space. If the cosmos is the self-expression of God and if the sun–planets system is the subsequent self-expression of the cosmos, then this planet and all others are the self-expression of God and, therefore, divine by their very beings.

The virginal conception of the cosmos becomes the virginal birth of the planet Earth. The Spirit, already fully manifest and present, expresses itself throughout the created order in its being and evolution. Earth becomes mother of Mary and Mary becomes mother of God. The Spirit, present as Earth, is present in every womb, of every species. Christ before time and Christ in time is the same Christ. When the soul of Jesus already present in Mary's womb began gathering the soil, water, and air to himself, the author of life, the author of the

Earth appeared as the person and body of Jesus Christ. Jesus is the life of God wrapped in flesh, his flesh drawn from the planet into Mary's womb. Mary's womb, then, is the planet Earth in miniature. With his and with every conception, the whole drama of evolution is played out again: God manifests divine life as unicellular, then multicellular, amphibian, mammalian, primate, and human. To ridicule or denigrate our evolutionary emergence is to ridicule and denigrate its creator! The womb is sacred habitat whether conception is through the exchange of the *BioLogos* (DNA) or directly by spirit. The same spirit is present in any case, the one Spirit of God.

The planet flows through us in every moment from conception through death and decomposition. In fact, that flow precedes our conception in that the male cell and female cell preceded our conception and were both sustained by the water, soil, and air in the bodies of both parents. So many people get confused about when life begins; it doesn't! Life is one; in fact, it is the One moving from unmanifest to manifest states. Conception and death are simply life's entry and exit from form. Following death, our physical forms return to their constituent organic compounds—"dust to dust." Life then reuses them in the creation of new life forms. Jesus of Nazareth was one such life form. We, like Jesus, are life itself and along with all that lives, we self-shape those organic compounds into bone, blood, muscle, and brain. Jesus of Nazareth is understood by Christians as being life itself. God's author of life itself! We are that life attempting to understand and experience its own identity. Jesus as ChristLogos was self-shaping the universe, which self-shaped the planet, which self-shaped Mary, who self-shaped him! Mary's womb (every womb) was sacred habitat in which the pre-existent God shaped his own body in existence. Again, life is one; lives are many. For Christian mystics, this planet is sacred because it manifests the life that is Christ. In John 14:6–7, Christ says as much:

> "I am the Way, and the truth and the life.
> No one can come to the Father except through me.

If you know me, you will know my Father too.
From this moment, you know him and have seen
him."

But what of the "descent among the dead"? What could that mean for the Christian mystic? We could say that each of us has a history that begins in God's infinite silence, emerges as universe through the ChristLogos, then appears as earth, unicellular life, multicellular life, marine organism, terrestrial amphibian, reptile, mammal, primate, and finally human. Human culture is the recent edge of the manifestation of the ChristLogos. All who went before us are considered "the dead." We can think of Jesus' descent as a journey "backward" down the tunnel of space/time to his origin in God. In doing so, he reopened or cleared our way "back" to our original selves. His return from the dead culminated in Resurrection on the third day. Thus he is the Way—he showed us the way into our depth, our infinite interior selves, to God. He is the Truth—the way to him results in the realization of truth: that we *ARE* him! He is the Life—that which we call our souls, our lives, is his soul, his life in the form that is our selves. Viewed in this way, destruction of the Earth escapes the categories of good and evil and must be understood as insanity! Cosmos and Earth are our unconscious selves. We are cosmos and Earth evolved into self-reflexive consciousness. Culture is the collective form of the self-reflection of Earth and cosmos, Earth and cosmos contemplating themselves. Earth and cosmos contemplating themselves is God thinking in matter. This is why all cultures begin with a holy book or a shaman as the holy book of preliterate cultures. Culture springs from religion (*religio,* to relink), God thinking about God in us, in the Earth, and in the cosmos.

CHAPTER 5

Life: The Sacrament of the Earth

The silence of God is the contemplation, the meditation of God. God has been meditating since pre-time, pre-space. The meditation of God is eternity! Space/time and energy/matter are themselves the evolving contemplation of God. In that we ourselves are creatures of space/time and energy/matter, we ourselves are the contemplation of God. So, when we meditate, we are just being ourselves, our real selves, our divine selves. When the heat of our real selves melts the thin structures of the egoic self, the space opened within is God's contemplation. Buddhists call this space *sunyata*. It is the silence of God within. So to contemplate is really our consent to allow God to contemplate us.

We need only do what Mary of Nazareth did. We need only yield to, say yes to, the spirit already present within us—the spirit that is us! When the dried crust of the egoic self falls away, the soul, the spirit within, is able to shine forth. Denied contents such as guilt, shame, and regret come tumbling out and the "lamp" within shines brightly. That spirit shining forth from within is our essential self, the soul, the fourth voice, the presence of the one God within. God is allowed to contemplate us into being again from our home in eternity. We can still say no! But saying no does not separate us from the Great Contemplation that is the universe. All it means is that we have returned to building the false self, the "bushel basket" to cover the lamp. We can deny the divinity of our true selves but that only denies our *experience* of our divinity. We remain, in our depth, divine nonetheless. Like the universe, we are sacramental.

So how, then, is life the sacrament of Earth? The planet is composed of a series of envelopes, each engulfing the one before it. The first is the core of the planet itself, hot and molten. Wrapped around it is the rock mantle, and around that the crust. Surrounding the external surface of the crust is the hydrosphere, the waters that nearly cover the Earth. Similarly, the atmosphere surrounds the whole planet and is itself layered in lighter and lighter envelopes going "up." The photosphere is the presence of sunlight permeating the atmosphere and the hydrosphere and all life forms. Also surrounding the planet's surface is the biosphere, the envelope of the whole life community.

Life is the boiling forth of the mind of God from energy and matter. Life is the internal or interior sensitivity of God welling up in forms. Life is one as God is one but the forms of life are many—thus the many life forms we see around and in us. That sensitivity first boils up as anaerobic and then aerobic cells. Next, it boils up as multicellular life forms and then as marine organisms. Life in the sea becomes life on the land as the amphibians evolve and crawl ashore. Next, the reptiles then the mammals then the primate and finally the human primate. In the human, the one life community becomes able to feel itself, feel its interior sentience, to contemplate itself. Within the human, the contemplation of God contemplates itself and sees that it is all good!

But there is a peril that comes with this human kind of consciousness. That peril is pretense, the ability to pretend, to imagine ourselves to be the contempla*tor,* the medita*tor,* the crea*tor!* While we are sacraments of the universe and Earth, we can pretend, imagine that we own them. We can pretend that we are separate "lives" rather than one life community. We can forget that we are life's consciousness able to be conscious of itself. We can forget that the life community is our "unconscious" mind, that Earth is a deeper "unconscious," and that the universe is the deepest dimension of ourselves. We can forget that we come from the divine silence of eternity, that we are that silence able to appreciate its own depth. When we do so, we can create false selves, pretentious selves, both individually as well as collectively. False selves serve false gods such as greed, power, consumerism, and many addictions. Then we become slaves to the addictions themselves. A shadow of pain and sorrow then eclipses our real selves, our real divine nature. That shadow, when joined to other shadows, forms another collective envelope around the Earth—the skotosphere, the sphere of shadows. The skotosphere is a collective false self; it is the skotosphere that is ruining the Earth. The skotosphere pollutes the heavenly presence of God, the ChristLogos, and makes it feel like hell itself. But it isn't hell; it is just a cloud blocking the light for a time. It can melt like a mist in the morning light.

Imagine one of those box-shaped cheese graters with a lighted candle at its center. Imagine that the grater is the material universe and the candlelight is consciousness. Imagine that we, each of us, is an empty space through which the radiance shines. The skotosphere is the darkness resulting from the blocking of those empty spaces. The light shines on within, but it is eclipsed in shadow. The false self, the pretend self, blocks the spaces through which the light of consciousness should shine, as many people are blocked these days because most Christians have abandoned the practice of deep confession. The Buddhists' sunyata (emptying) has its equivalent in Christian confession or in Jewish Yom Kippur (atonement). When we discuss the rites further on, we will discuss this emptying function.

"Nature mysticism" is the practice of meditating with life, as life, by allowing the self-boundary to yield to the larger truth that our life is life itself, the boiling over of spirit from within matter. Another way to say it is that nature is being contemplated into existence by spirit. We realize that we *ARE* nature, we *ARE* life, we *ARE* spirit. Buddhist mysticism, Taoist mysticism, and Hindu mysticism have different names for spirit: Mind, Tao, Brahman, respectively. They are different names for The One and not different "Ones." Were they different Ones, they would not be The One. The mission for Christians is to discover (take the covering off) the presence of The One, the

ChristLogos in each person. The mission for Buddhists, Taoists, and Hindus is to discover Mind, Tao, and Brahman in the ChristLogos. Only this mutual discovery will provide an adequate basis for intercultural peace.

Jesus Christ was a member of the life community that he contemplated into being. In realizing his oneness with and as The One, he spoke as the life community, as the Earth, as the cosmos, and as the pre-existent being whence they emerged. On hearing him, people remarked that, unlike the scribes and Pharisees (exoteric religious functionaries), he spoke with authority. How could he not speak with authority? He was the author! Being emptied of his egoic self, he realized his divine personhood. His emptiness (sunyata) spoken of by St. Paul was the source of his authority. Offspring of God, he spoke as God's being.

Although identified with authorship of the whole creation, Jesus, like each of us, was a human being within it. He was one of the many that are The One. Jesus, emptied of himself, opened to the wisdom of his Father. Then, speaking as himself, he could speak with the whole architecture of his soul. The whole architecture of his soul *IS* the cosmos! We, each of us, are also that same architecture, that same soul, that same self. We need only empty ourselves and remember who we are.

Jesus of Nazareth was a male mammal born of a female mammal. He entered his own creation in the ocean womb of a woman. From within, he gathered the water, air, and soil of creation and fashioned from them blood, flesh, and bone of his body. This is the same body that, as we noted earlier, would die torn and tortured on the cross. He who engendered the cosmos entered into it materially by the sacrament of Annunciation or conception. In the sacrament of Nativity, he moved down the birth canal of another mammal. In doing so, he emerged as did we with the same expectations of welcome, warmth, of milk and love. He felt that warmth pressed against the breasts and belly of his mammalian mother. He tugged at and sucked on her nipples for the much-needed milk. He heard again and felt again the heaving breath and heartbeat of her young heart. Perhaps he felt her generosity—"take, drink, this is my body"! That same breathing and heartbeat went on drumming through the whole nine months of his ocean home in her body. Later he would hear those same rhythms in the music of his Jewish people. He would dance to those same rhythms at weddings and celebrations. Jesus, like us, was a mammal; Jesus had the mammalian experience. It is therefore holy to be a mammal.

CHAPTER 6

Culture: The Sacrament of Life

"And there are other sheep I have
that are not of this fold
and I must lead these too.
They too will listen to my voice,
and there will be only one flock,
one Shepherd."

JOHN 10:16

From the silent consciousness of God energy emerged and then matter. From matter came living cells, organisms, sea and land animals, birds and insects, grasses and flowers. In time the reptiles emerged and then the basal mammals and from them the primates. From the primates came humans and from humans came culture. Human self-reflection provided a space, a venue in which the Christ-Logos could become aware of itself within matter. This is the true meaning of incarnation: God awakening in matter. Cultures are by their very natures sacred in that they express in human society the inherent presence of God. Fascism, communism, and all tyrannies that deny the presence of God sooner or later cease to be. The same fate awaits biocidal cultures that deny the presence of God in the life community that they plunder.

Archaeology reveals to us that the earliest expressions of human cultures exhibit a search to understand the source of the human. This search is the expression of our need to understand the meaning of our existence and destiny. If in our depth we are the presence of God, all of us, then the search is God's awakening to the divine presence within us! Evolution is a search for ever more complex forms of life so that God can finally evolve a brain complex enough to realize the divine identity in matter, in flesh. And there does seem to be built into the very structure of our brains the need to identify with a larger, more sacred identity. For Christians, with the realization that Christ is the evolving creativity of God, it then follows that we realize that the cosmos, Earth, and the life community, including all human cultures, are also expressions of this creativity. All cultures seek to know and experience and therefore to understand the workings of the sacred. All cultures participate in the presence of the one divine life, expressed in the one life community. For the Christian, the sacred mission of our time is to identify the presence of the ChristLogos in other cultures by whatever name it is called in those cultures. Every culture has a word for love and they all point to the same experience. In other words, we must accept the sheep "not of this fold" as brothers and sisters of the One Flock.

I mentioned earlier that Jesus entered into space/time through the womb and birth canal of a woman. Like all of us, he was born amidst blood and pain. and he would die amidst blood and pain. The cosmos is said to have come forth in a spontaneous eruption of space and time. In a similar "virgin birth," Jesus is said to have simply appeared in his mother's womb. In the sacrament of his Annunciation, his conception, he recreated the universe. Following conception, he reenacted the whole life story of evolution, unicellular to multicellular, multicellular to organism, to fish, amphibian, reptile, mammal, and primate, and then emerged into Hebrew culture. In his emergence into a culture, he gathered up all of cultural evolution from tribal and shamanic cultures, neolithic cultures, the great religious cultures, and all of those not of the Hebrew fold. If we are to call ourselves his followers, we must do the same. Christian mysticism is the experiential gathering of all cultures, all of life, the whole Earth and universe into

our memory and experience. How? By an ascension of consciousness sufficient to allow our brains to think with the mind of God as
ChristLogos. In the Persian religion of Zoroastrianism, God (called
Ahura Mazda) is said to contain and hold all being in his mind. For
the true Christian mystic, the experience of being held in the mind
of God leads to the experience of being one with the mind of God.
Throw a sponge in any body of water. While the sponge is held
by the water, the water is also in the sponge. The water is having a
sponge experience; the sponge is having a water experience. Christian mysticism is the remembering of all of space/time (the sponge)
and the source of space/time (the water). This remembering is the
meaning of our existence and that meaning reveals our equally sacred
destiny.

Cultures, like individuals, possess three dimensions or aspects of
their being. First, they have a differentiated outside that gives them
their differentness from other cultures. Second, they have an interior
sentience or sensitivity that shares human similarities with other cultures. Third, they share in the oneness that is human global culture as
a whole, as a single phenomenon of the life community of Earth. For
Christian mystics it is the second, the interior sentience, that can be
recognized as the ChristLogos though called by many other names.
For instance, Hindus might call it Visnu (the preserver) or Taoists
might call it Tao, and Buddhists might call it Mind. Why would anyone want to believe that unless water has been splashed on your head
with a form of words that God will condemn you to some eternal
hell? Is God some sort of cosmic Joseph Mengele willing to shovel
India, China, and Africa into a burning pit? Who would insult God in
this way? Those who create such a monstrous and neurotic God create him in their own image and likeness! No mature Christian could
hold such a belief. No one who experiences God through mysticism
could suffer from such insanity.

As noted, individuals too have a three-fold nature. I am this particular being called Albert, unique and differentiated from you and

from all others. This self is the self of this particular organism and so I call it the "organic self." There is also an interior or sentient self (the water within the sponge), which I experience as my self or soul. Through meditation, Eucharist, and prayer, I have come to see that this self or soul is an expression of a much larger soul (the water that holds the sponge) and that in my essence, I *AM* that larger soul, the ChristLogos! And so are you, the reader, by whatever name you refer to the "essential self." Stated simply, I'm me and you are you. We both experience an interior sentience that is nonlocal and is One—The One.

This essential self is deeper than the organic self, the self of this organism, or of the egoic self, the self that I think I am. It is that in which the organism abides. The organism dwells in time and space; it has a beginning, a middle, and an end. The essential self is the presence of God contemplating the universe into being. The essential self is the local presentation of the nonlocal life of God, the Spirit or ChristLogos. It is existence itself, and we are existents within it. Each organic self, whether the self of a tree, a dinosaur, or a giraffe, emerges as a new local expression of this soul of souls. What human being, what human culture could NOT be a presentation of the ChristLogos by whatever name? When the Christian mystic reaches out to understand this interior sentience in those of other cultures, he or she reaches out to Christ.

As the whole, this essential self or ChristLogos has existed in every culture at every moment since the dawn of time. Time and space, to repeat, are products of this self. We can imagine ourselves as a node on a vast energy web, "tapped in" to the larger energy system. When we experience our oneness with the ChristLogos we unite our organic selves with his essential self, his presence in all cultures, at all times, in a supreme experience of unitive spirituality. Mysticism unites us with an experience that transcends all cultures, all languages, all names of God—and still includes them all in itself. Whatever the name used to name the transcendent One, we experience identity with that One across all cultural boundaries. That unitive experience transcends culture itself and awakens our unitive experience with the whole life community. The unitive experience with all of life leads to the unitive experience with Earth, the universe, and eternity itself. We cross over the event horizon of space/time and *KNOW* our own unitive truth with the living God.

PART II

Unitive Prayer

A Note on Unitive Prayer

Certain themes will be repeated again and again throughout this book. The reason is that basic unitive themes must be applied again and again to different aspects of Christian life and practice. As noted earlier, there are three modalities or domains of God's presence. First, there is God's unmanifest dimension, which we have called the Father. The outer edge of this unmanifest dimension is an infinite silence, an infinite no-thingness. From this silent no-thingness, the manifest domain of God's presence emerges and grows or evolves. We can call this manifestation the Son of the Father. Third, in all manifest expressions of The One are the sentient many. This sentience is the interior ChristLogos, or Spirit. As one of these many, what the Taoists call "the myriad things," we pray as the Son to the Father. Most prayers are of this nature: prayers to the Father. Unitive prayer is the prayer of silence, praying *AS* the Father in the unitive experience of the unmanifest, the manifest, and sentient as The One.

Mysticism *IS* the practice of oneness *with* God rather than praying *to* God as though we were somehow separate. While we are not separate from God, neither are any of us the fullness of God. Again, the sponge metaphor: we possess within a measure of the fullness of the ocean that nonetheless is not separate from the ocean. Now, there is nothing bad or immature about praying to God. This whole book is one such prayer! But if we wish to be unitive with all cultures, all life forms, Earth, the cosmos, the silence and presence of God, we must listen to that silence *as* that silence. Meditation is the practice of unitive prayer. We are all surprised to find out what can be heard from and as silence. When there are no words, thoughts, concepts, or images, no singing or chanting, we hear The One behind the origin of things. When we become God's silence, we begin to hear the still deeper voice of the Father. When we become aware of this, we know what Jesus meant when he proclaimed oneness with the Father.

CHAPTER 7

The Magnificat

Authentic spirituality can be summed up in one word: *surrender.* In surrender, we give up on the will of our small, egoic selves. We yield that will in order to open to a far deeper will, the will of God. We, as manifest creation, allow ourselves to be split open, in order to birth the unmanifest divine will. I think this intention motivates many who "claim Jesus as their personal Lord and Savior" and then claim "rebirth" following the voicing of that claim. The danger is that it is the egoic self itself that is making the claim, causing the little self to inflate rather than to shrink or desiccate. Egoism is easy enough to spot; it feels manipulative. The Magnificat, Mary's yes to God, is the finest example of true surrender to the divine. So deep was this surrender that the divine took on flesh in her womb! Mary's yes, an unqualified yes, allowed the Incarnation to become. Her will was presumably free, like ours, to choose to say no. One shudders to imagine what Mary's no would have meant!

Surrender is the letting go of what we know in order to be in touch with the source of knowing itself. We let go of what we think in order that a mind greater than our own might think within us. We let go of what we feel in order to feel the sentience of the whole. We allow our instincts to inform us in our depth, to signal truth to our feelings and thoughts. Surrender allows the human brain, itself a creation of consciousness, to become the vehicle of higher and higher states of consciousness. Each time we surrender the mind with which we think, we inherit a higher mind with which to think. We come to see that the brain is merely the site of reception and transmission of consciousness, of the ChristLogos. So let us begin the Christian story with Mary's surrender, Mary's yes, the Annunciation. From Luke 1:46–55, Mary said to Elizabeth:

> "My soul magnifies the Lord,
> and my spirit rejoices in God my Savior,
> for he has looked with favor on the lowliness of his
> servant.
> Surely, from now on all generations will call me
> blessed;
> For the Mighty One has done great things for me,
> and holy is his name.
> His mercy is for those who fear him
> from generation to generation.
> He has shown strength with his arm;
> he has scattered the proud in the thoughts of their
> hearts.
> He has brought down the powerful from their
> thrones,
> and lifted up the lowly;
> he has filled the hungry with good things,
> and sent the rich away empty.
> He has helped his servant Israel,
> in remembrance of his mercy,
> according to the promise he made to our ancestors,
> to Abraham and to his descendants forever."

When we look through the unitive lens, the poem renders beautiful meanings. Let's look together, line by line.

"My soul magnifies the Lord." Any who have truly surrendered the little, egoic self experience in the wake of that surrender a profound magnification of joy, an expansion of consciousness and being. The egoic self then seems a cramped prison for the soul. With the surrender and subsequent shattering of the small self, we feel like Lazarus walking out from his tomb. We enter into an experience of expansion, co-extensive with life, with Earth, and with the universe. Buddhists call this *Nam myoho renge kyo:* "My soul and the soul of the universe are one soul." Mary's soul felt the magnification of her soul in that way. Suddenly, she embodied the ChristLogos who had created her!

"And my spirit rejoices in God my Savior." Until one has experienced surrender, it is difficult if not impossible to imagine the upwelling of joy in the interior of one's self, just released from the prison of being a self-in-miniature. One experiences the expansive wonder of who we really are! Mary reports that in the magnification of her soul she felt "saved." Saved from what? From the lifelong prison of a miserable and shrunken existence. Unfortunately, most people accept that misery as being without an option. Mary's option was to embody God. Ours is the same.

"Surely, from now on all generations will call me blessed." What greater blessing could one receive than pregnancy of any kind, let alone to be the mother of eternity itself? Any pregnancy, human or animal, is just that—mothering eternity! But what could it have meant to embody the incarnate author of the universe that you yourself are an expression of? And to know it?! Every act of eating, drinking, and breathing brought to the developing child the planetary nutrients created by him that were now creating him!

"For the Mighty One has done great things for me and holy is his name." The root of the word *holy* is the Greek word *holos,* which means "whole or complete." Mary was articulating something far deeper than self-indulgent pieties. She was articulating that the name of God is "whole." ("I am who am" = being itself.) The whole is the Mighty One, the All Powerful One of whom we are the many. Truly, the Mighty One did do great things for her!

"His mercy is for those who fear him from generation to generation." Jesus, the incarnate ChristLogos, has been called the incarnation of God's mercy. An honest reading of the Hebrew Bible, or Old Testament, provides justification enough for truly fearing God! But Mary was not talking about emotional fear or terror. What she meant was closer to the word *awe*. Awe is an inward response to the stunning presence and truth, the tenderness and mercy, the intimacy of the Mighty One who is God. Mary, pregnant, is the very symbol of unitive spirituality, in that the presence of God was emerging within her very being. I am dictating this book to my pregnant daughter, Rebecca, who carries within her her first child, my first grandchild. Her mother Carol's pregnancy for Becky and for her sister Kateri were the supreme moments of my spiritual life. Through the mystical lens, no pregnancies are any less miraculous, any less divine than that of Mary.

"He has shown strength with his arm; he has scattered the proud in the thoughts of their hearts." The *scattering* of the proud of thought, the conceited, is really the *shattering* of the false, egoic self. As already noted, this scattering/shattering dynamic is the logical result of surrender. The avoidance of this dynamic leads to so many tragedies. Step Three is the surrender step in all Twelve Step programs such as that of Alcoholics Anonymous. The addict self must die, must shatter, for the real, the essential self, to emerge. In John 3:30, the Baptist points to this in saying of himself and Jesus, "He must grow greater, I must grow less."

"He has brought down the powerful from their thrones, and lifted up the lowly." As I write this book, we Americans grieve the passing of President Gerald Ford. President Ford in his decency, his humility, was "lifted up" to the presidency of this great nation. The pride of the "powerful" pulled them from office, leaving them humiliated for all time. This was true not only for President Nixon but for Vice President Agnew as well. Never elected to either office, Gerald Ford, this man of deep faith, found himself called to heal the divisions of the nation. These incidents are examples of what Mary was talking about, events that magnify the power of God.

"He has filled the hungry with good things, and sent the rich away empty." Greed leads "the rich" to attempt to fill their spiritual emptiness (not emptiness or sunyata in the Buddhist sense) with addictive substances and behaviors. Whether greed, power, pleasure, or intoxication, all and any such false gods lead eventually to the slavery of addiction. All addiction is like drinking sea water—cool and satisfying at first swallow, it soon becomes a burning rage in the body. It will lead in the end to madness and death. In third-millennium Christianity, we must talk more about addiction than about sin, the behaviors of addiction. If we need to be redeemed, and I myself did, it is from addiction and not from "missing the mark," the Hebrew meaning of the word *sin*. More on that later.

"He has helped his servant Israel, in remembrance of his mercy, according to the promise he made to our ancestors, to Abraham and to his descendants forever." The mission of the true Christian mystic is to expand the understanding or meaning of "the descendants of Abraham," certainly to all Jews and Muslims, but now to others as well. These others are his "other folds" that have to be under one shepherd. As mentioned earlier, the mission of modern Christian mystics is to discover the interior sentience present in all faiths. In this interiority, we experience the ChristLogos in these others, and thus meet Christ in them. To be a "missionary" will now mean to go to other cultures and learn from them how to identify this interior sentience in their approach to the "transcendent One." Then, having done so, we return to our Christian communities to educate them as to how the ChristLogos is present in the "other flocks of Christ." Put simply, we travel to others to learn rather than to teach. We return to our own in order to teach.

CHAPTER 8

The Jungian Rosary

The great psychologist C. G. Jung, student of Sigmund Freud, set in motion a very powerful movement in the field of psychology, spirituality, and mythology that can be called Jungian psychology. One of the great Jungian mythologists, among several, was Joseph Campbell. Campbell is to mythology what Einstein is to physics. In his greatest book, *The Hero with a Thousand Faces,* he showed the universal oneness of the mythologies of the world, which is behind and supports their apparent differences. He created a convincing model that showed the transcendent, the cosmic, and the individual nature of all these sacred stories. His reader is left with a sense that the various cultures are just different languages of God.

The Roman Catholic rosary illustrates this "hero journey" in the story of Mary/Christ. All major cultures have some form of rosary bead worship, for prayer, for chanting, or for meditation. Christianity has this rosary, which I am calling the Jungian rosary. For those readers who are unfamiliar with the rosary and how to pray it, a quick trip to any Catholic bookstore will provide many books and pamphlets on the beads. While any one of them can adequately explain the mechanics of this great feminine prayer, none provides the following explanation of its use as a mystical Christian tool. We could think of the following as praying the rosary as a third-millennium Christian.

The Joyful Mysteries

There are fifteen "mysteries" or pictures in the whole rosary. The first five are called Joyful, the next five Sorrowful, and the final five Glorious. As noted in the preceding chapter, the whole Christian story began with the triumphant "yes!" of Mary in her Magnificat. The Magnificat was her joyful response to the Annunciation made to her by an angel (Greek: *angelos,* or messenger) of God. The Annunciation, thus the first of all sacraments, is the meeting place between time and eternity. Time and eternity intersect in the womb of a woman. God conceived as a mammal! God conceived as a primate! God made incarnate (embodied) in the life community itself a creation of the divine self. To use Campbell's term, the Annunciation is the "call to adventure." First Mary and then Jesus entered into an adventure that neither of them could have fully comprehended in advance. This is the first Joyful Mystery.

Mary next paid a visit to her cousin Elizabeth, who was also pregnant. Elizabeth was carrying John the Baptist, the last of the great Hebrew prophets ("last" for Christians, at least). Mary needed Elizabeth to confirm and validate Mary's divine calling; Elizabeth did so and then John leapt in her womb! Elizabeth here represents the spiritual community supporting or supposing to support the adventure. Too often, the community—shriveled, dogmatic, and angry—represents the greatest obstacle to the one called to adventure. Among mystics, the function of validation is more likely to occur regardless of the tradition the mystic is from. So, like young pregnant women in any age, Mary and Elizabeth shared their joys and fears. This is the second Joyful Mystery.

Up to this point, the "Christian story" is the story of women, Jewish women. The third Joyful Mystery is called the Nativity, the sacrament of birth. Interestingly enough, the drama of birth is played out in a stable, among other species of mammals. The infant ChristLogos, having repeated *in utero* all stages of life, from unicellular through mammal/primate, now transitions from an aquatic to an air-breathing terrestrial being. Here the story of Jesus truly begins. God, transcendent of the cosmos, emergent in the cosmos, is now an individual human sleeping in a grain trough, warmed by the breath of cattle.

It occurred to me, as I wrote this, that the Christian season of Advent is a commemoration of the gestation of Jesus. Christmas is Campbell's "birth of the hero." It is said that Hindu and Zoroastrian mystics made the long trip to honor this hero of heroes. The grown Jesus would later teach his disciples, saying, "Anyone who is not against us is for us" (Mark 9:40). The Eastern mystics of any tradition have never been against Jesus or against us, for that matter. In fact, there is increasing evidence that Jesus studied with them during his unrecorded absence of seventeen years.

The fourth Joyful Mystery, called the Circumcision, is more accurately named Baptism for Christians. It represents the *ex utero* welcome into the community in which Jesus was already embedded by being in Mary's womb, or habitat. The community is the new and larger habitat, embracing the life of the newborn. In patrifocal religions such as Christianity, Judaism, and Islam, this also represents a passing from the feminine into the world of the masculine.

It is among the men, among the "doctors" of Jewish law, that we find Jesus in the fifth Joyful Mystery called the Finding in the Temple. This event is recalled in the Christian initiation called Confirmation, though much of its power has presently drained out of it. In the temple, the hero has entered "the world."

The Sorrowful Mysteries

The first of these five mysteries is called the Agony in the Garden. At this stage, the hero begins to grasp, to realize (make real) the monstrous pain of the world. What up until now seemed a noble and generous call to truth, now seems to become despair tinged with terror. Self-doubt howls mockingly within. Those who avoided this road by embedding themselves in whatever roles the world offers seem to have made the saner choice. But there is no way back; the way of pain seems inevitable.

We now arrive at the second Sorrowful Mystery, the Scouring at the Pillar. The scourging commemorates the whipping of Jesus with the Roman cat-o-nine-tails. This stage of the journey is about dealing with the demands of the body and the yearnings of the soul. The male body cries out for the comfort of the feminine, the comfort seemingly reserved now for those who have stayed in the safety of the culture as it is. Flames of loneliness and the barbs of a thousand needles sting and claw at the body of flesh. Whatever the hero imagined he was doing now seems absurd, insane.

This opens the door to the third Sorrowful Mystery, the Crowning with Thorns. The head, the seat of cognition, must now be transcended. The time of death has come to the self we knew ourselves to be, the shallow egoic self. This is the self we constructed from our thoughts about ourselves and out of others' opinions of us. The ego collapses, shatters as the hero feels more and more the fool before those who know and/or love him. Egoic thought must be transcended or genuine madness will ensue. As T. S. Eliot once said, "The cost will be not less than everything." When the loss of everything is accepted, the journey can continue.

The fourth Sorrowful Mystery is the Carrying of the Cross. Gone is community support, the respect of friends, even one's idea of oneself. Weakened, there are falls along the way, feelings of cowardice, self-hatred, and shame. There is a deep desire to abandon the foolishness and scurry back into the safety of the world. There is still death awaiting.

Crucifixion means death. This fifth Sorrowful Mystery, Crucifixion, represents the death of the hero's idea of himself as well as his idea of God. "God," the originator of "the call," seems to turn his back, casting the hero into shadow, complete darkness. Only complete disgust can cause us to forsake all others. "God" seems to join the tormentors in disgust for the hero. Even the presence of "God," whom the hero thought he was upholding and serving, is absent now; even "God" has walked away! Jesus cries out, "Why have you forsaken me?" Death is now complete.

The Glorious Mysteries

But God didn't die, nor was God disgusted. God abandons no one. What died was the idea of God, a mental construct inherited from the culture, from the world. Resurrection is the explosive awakening of the actual, the true spirit or self of God within the hero. Resurrection is the first of the Glorious Mysteries. Each of us is an individual and around that individuality the egoic self was created. Each of us has an organic self as an expression of the cosmos, the creation, this individual organism. Each of us also has an essential self, the birthless and deathless ChristLogos within. Resurrection is the magnification, the expression of this essential and divine self. This essential self arises in the empty tomb, left behind by the egoic self. The empty tomb is now an Earth-womb, birth canal for the eternal. Resurrection is the expression of the God-self within every creature, the very life of God. Easter is the welling up of God unmanifest now made manifest. I mentioned earlier the Buddhist teaching *Nam myoho renge kyo:* "The self of the universe and my self are the same self." Resurrection goes further: my self, the universe self, and the eternal self are the same self! The baby in the stable—the carpenter's son, the awakened teacher, the fool who lost everything for Truth, who bore the grinning stupidities of the world—has now become the very life of God present in an ascended, transfigured, glorified body. The transfigured brain, now able to accommodate and think with the mind of God, has ascended into supreme consciousness.

The second of the Glorious Mysteries is this Ascension. Made light by and made into light by the Resurrection and Ascension, the hero enters into the male pregnancy. What appears to be a man now carries the eternal within; space/time and life are pregnant with the eternal. Thinking with and as the mind of God, the ChristLogos awakens to awareness of itself, its true identity, its divinity. The hero is now pregnant with the very spirit that engendered him.

The third Glorious Mystery is the descent of the Holy Spirit, the birthing of God into the world. The hero has given birth to eternity in time so that space/time could recognize its real and divine identity. Consciousness equals $E = mc^2$. In the gift of the Holy Spirit, the hero has opened a tired world to the springtime of God. God, divine husband, can wed again his planetary bride and life can be born again, made sacred again. In so doing, the "bride" assumes the same divinity as her maker.

This Assumption is the fourth Glorious Mystery. We are in the feminine again, but a transcendent and enlightened one, joined to a transcendent and enlightened masculine. All is whole again, holy again!

And so, in the fifth, the final Glorious Mystery, the Coronation of Mary as queen of heaven, it becomes clear that Mary has given birth to the hero that is herself. In the fairy tales, he becomes king and she is crowned queen; Earth is joined again to heaven and all is sacred. This is the new heaven and new Earth of both Christian and Buddhist prophecies. The whole feminine truth of her womb/habitat, Earth/habitat, and her cosmos, the womb of God, is now the queen of happiness in a world made new, a new Eden in a paradise regained.

CHAPTER 9

The Lord's Prayer

As its title indicates, this prayer (outlined by Jesus in Matthew 6:9–15) is for Christians, the prayer of the Lord himself. As such, it possesses a special weight and relevance to any and all Christians. The Lord's Prayer is what he himself has directed us to do in praying. It begins with the words "Our Father." What it does not say is "My Father" or "Father of all Christians." It represents the welcoming embrace of all, the inclusion of everyone in the prayer of everyone. Continuing:

"Our Father who art in Heaven." Awakening results from an evolution from "below" as an "involution" from above. From below, the sequence is matter to life to mind; from above, being to consciousness to bliss. They intersect in the enlightened person, the one risen or prepared to receive the rebirth from above. Heaven is that ineffable state wherein only God fully knows God. We cannot know God as God knows God, completely. In our finitude, whatever we know, there is always more to know, an infinite more to know. We do know something of God as Father, Son, and Spirit. We know that God is our source, our Father, or Father and Source of us all.

"Hallowed be thy Name." All cultures seek to understand the source, The One, and call that One by many names. The name is not The One; it is a name for The One. The One remains mysterious, ineffable, undifferentiated though still the source of the many. In the Hebrew/Christian Bible, the prophet/mystic Moses realizes the name of God as being—"I am who am," says The One through the

47

soul of a bush. "I am being itself." Cultures are all collective attempts to name and understand and know being.

"Thy kingdom come." The kingdom of God is the unimpeded presence of God, eternal being in time. Jesus says that that kingdom is not of this world. He also says that his kingdom can be found in our midst! In true surrender, the silence, the stillness, the emptiness of the unmanifest, eternal God becomes manifest among us. We are then not of this world, though still in this world; we are the eternal present in time.

"Thy will be done." The eternal, present in time, then redeems time, suffusing it with eternity. The eternal unmanifest made into the manifest *IS* the will of God. The will that willed the universe, Earth, life, and culture into being is the same will that also sustains the cosmos, Earth, life, and culture—the same will is made incarnate in Mary's womb, as the Father, the Spirit, and the Son. The inherent laws of the universe—gravity, electromagnetism, and the two nuclear forces—as well as the organizational ecology of the whole biosphere and the moral guidelines of cultures, are all expressions of that one will. This can only be known by yielding one's will to the greater will of God. "Thy will be done" is the mantra for all mystics, and certainly for Christian mystics. It comes down to this: "My life is none of my business."

"On earth … ." To ask that God's will be done on Earth, on this plane of existence, begs a question: What is God's will for Earth? Life is God's will for Earth! In Genesis, the whole creation is found to be good and the human very good. Did God not will life for insects, plants, birds, animals, *and* for humankind? Did God not will soil, rocks, mountains, streams, rivers, clouds, oceans, lakes, storms, and seasons into being? Is it not therefore the central responsibility for all Christians to open to God's will on Earth? The idea that Christians can remain indifferent to life on Earth and still be Christians is the moral equivalent of leprosy. That leprosy spreads corruption through the life community, the creation of God, of God as ChristLogos.

"As it is in heaven." As it is in the mysterious self-knowledge of God. If God's will brought forth and is the will behind evolution, then our request in this prayer is that our yielded egos will be replaced by that same will of God. Our wills, then, are to be venues for the will of heaven, of eternity. Indeed, the conforming of our will to the more profound will of God is the only proper use of our will in any case. Inherent in all of this is our spiritual responsibility toward all that lives on Earth, for that was his will in Genesis. Christianity is spiritual ecology; Christianity is God's will on Earth, for all of life, and for all cultures.

"Give us this day … ." I once read somewhere that Mahatma Gandhi once said something like the following: "If we have more than what we need we have stolen it from the poor." If we really did only take what we need, no one would starve today. The insects, plants, birds, and animals would not be going extinct, the rainforests would be left intact. Again, what is God's will on Earth as it is in heaven? Life! Remember, the prayer began with the word "our," not "my." And why "this day"? Elsewhere, Jesus taught to take no thought of tomorrow, that tomorrow would care for itself (Matthew 6:34). Living in this day means living in the Now—and in the eternal Now is where God lives. Because God is eternity in time, we meet God now or not at all.

"Our daily bread." Again, "our," not "my" daily bread, and not bread for my culture only. What is being affirmed here is everyone's need—and everyone's right—to eat. Buddha said that hunger is the greatest of all sufferings. When we insist upon individual and collective gluttony, we inflict that suffering on others. To destroy their habitat for reasons of human greed does the same to other species. Asking for "our bread" is to ask for the bread for us all.

"Forgive us our trespasses." We trespass on each other, on each other's cultures. We trespass on the habitat of plants and animals, of the pre-born, and we are in need, all of us, of constant and continual forgiveness of these trespasses. We are also trespassed upon, violated, abused, insulted, exploited, and, like Jesus, murdered.

"As we forgive those who trespass against us." And we must forgive in order to heal. The alternative to true forgiveness is a life of resentment. Resentment leads inevitably to fear, to addiction, and to a general malaise of the soul. When I say this part of the prayer, I sometimes change it slightly. I say, "Help us to forgive those who trespass against us," because forgiveness is so very difficult.

"Lead us not into temptation." The only real temptation for the mystic is to take back his or her will. I have heard the word *ego* used as an acronym for Easing God Out. When I once again focus on my will, the will of the egoic self, the greater will of God is eclipsed, impeded in its movement. Because pain is always the result, we are asking God for help to avoid reclaiming our own will over God's. When we fail, we simply surrender again.

"Deliver us from evil." When we rescind our surrender and kneel before our egos once again, we are immediately open to all forms of evil. In this part of the prayer, we are asking for help: "Please deliver us from doing evils as well as from being victimized by evil." Mostly, deliver us from the evil of lying to ourselves again, from building a false self again, from living in hell again.

"For thine is the kingdom." We return to our recognition that the "kingdom in our midst" is God, is the ChristLogos, is the Spirit! We acknowledge that this kingdom is our source, the source of the entire manifest universe, that the Kingdom is the whole cosmos, the whole Earth, the whole life community, and the whole community of humans. This acknowledgment is another surrender, another opening of our own essential selves.

"And the power … ." Another recognition that the will and creativity behind all evolution is the will, the creativity, the power of God. That power is the ever-present, ever-growing Spirit of God at every level, from the quantum and atomic to the galactic and universal. That power in Christian mystics results from our surrender. Surrender of ego-power enables us to become expressions of that power which is the will of the living and emergent God.

"And the glory … ." The beauty of the created order, the depth and glory of the night sky, the thundering expansion of the cosmos, the flight of the eagle, the breaching of the whale, the leap of the cat, the throbbing hooves of the horse, the presence of the beating heart, breath, and love are all the glory and the beauty of God.

"For ever and ever." From pre-time, during time, and following time, the kingdom, the power, and the glory are all the very presence of our eternal source, our God, our destiny. And we will not withdraw from surrender.

"Amen." *Amen,* chanted AAAA-MEN, is the Western equivalent of the Eastern Om (A–U–M). It is also an assertion that all the foregoing is true and lasting. Amen and Om are the sounds of God's presence throughout the multi-level universe. Amen is our commitment!

CHAPTER 10

The Creed

Throughout their history, Christians have formulated statements of faith. Most famous among these are the Apostles' Creed and later the Nicene Creed. The presentation following is a synthesis of the two, interpreted or explained through our unitive lens.

"We believe in one God, ..." The great reaffirmation of monotheism expressed for all time in the Jewish *Shema:* "Hear, O Israel, the Lord our God is One." *One* God, creator of the *uni*-verse. The universe, created of nothing but God's own being! The opening statement is clear, simple, and profound, not unlike the beginning of Beethoven's Fifth Symphony.

"The Father, ..." Jesus revealed God as *Abba,* Hebrew for Papa, a concerned parent, source of our individual and collective personhood.

"The Almighty, ..." This Papa/God is creator and sustainer of all that is, the source and destiny of everything and somehow of everyone. Papa is also the "presence" within all that is present, the "truth" in all that is true, the "beauty" in all that is beautiful. Because the universe is itself an expression of God's oneness, everything in the universe is somehow an expression of God's own being.

"Maker of heaven ... ." Heaven is a translation of the Greek word *ouranos,* which means "the heavens" or cosmos. With Jesus' statement that the kingdom of heaven is in our midst, we could also say that we are in the midst of heaven. For the mystic, heaven is more a level of awareness than a place to go to after death. In other words, we are already here; our job is to realize that fact.

"And earth, … ." Once again, Earth is clearly understood to be created of God, and therefore, sacred. Another name for Christian mystics could be "Christian ecologists" in that we understand the sacramental nature of Earth. In the next section of this book, we shall look at the unitive rites that underscore this truth.

"Of all that is, seen and unseen." What is seen is the material universe. What is unseen is the law expressed through that universe from gravity to ecological law to the omnipresence of love.

"We believe in one Lord, Jesus Christ, … ." A statement of faith in the message of the gospels. For mystics, it is also an expression of the goal of achieving the Christ-nature ourselves. To believe in Jesus Christ is to desire and to strive to achieve his nature through the process of surrender of our wills to the will of God.

"The only son of God, … ." This statement creates problems for many people, mostly due to a lack of unitive understanding. While we have emphasized the gospel of John in this book, usually the synoptics ("same-view") are more heavily quoted by less unitive writers. If Jesus was the incarnation of the ChristLogos, then the entire manifest universe (again, *ouranos*) is his being. Because all of us are differentiated expressions of the one ChristLogos/universe, then we too *are* the only Son, we too *are* the Christ.

"Eternally begotten of the Father, … ." The creative dynamics of the Father's own eternal being, emergent as space/time.

"God from God, … ." Not two Gods, but two dimensions of one God, the Spirit present prior to and within creation being the third dimension of the one God.

"Light from light, … ." God is the light of consciousness. As noted, consciousness is $E = mc^2$. Light emanating from light as sunlight emanates from the sun. The sun is a Trinity: first, the star we call the sun, second, the radiance of that star, and third, the warmth of that radiance! Jesus was light manifest from light unmanifest; we are as well.

"True God from true God, … ." Repeated again to be sure there is no confusion! As I mentioned earlier in the water-ice-steam analogy, and just now as the star-radiance-warmth analogy, one God expressed in three forms or dynamisms. One God, one light, one being in a sequence of transformations becoming universe, Earth, life, and culture.

"Begotten, not made, … ." Of one another and not created by one another.

"Of one being with the Father." Repeated yet again. Jesus Christ (and each of us) has the same essence or being as the Father and the Holy Spirit. God the Father is being itself or is-ness prior to manifestation. God the Holy Spirit is the Father's omnipresence throughout the created order. God the Son is the same is-ness, the same being flesh.

"Through him all things were made." Through his being as ChristLogos the universe came to be. The ChristLogos of the Father preceded space, time, energy, and matter. Space/time and energy/matter came into being through the ChristLogos. Jesus Christ is that creativity of the Father walking among us. Christ as Logos is the "stuff" of which the universe came to be. We too are that stuff!

"For us and for our salvation … ." He appeared as flesh in order to make us aware that flesh is an expression of divinity and permeated with it. Salvation (being saved) is achieved by waking up, by spiritual awakening to the truth of who we are. Who are we, then? We are the ChristLogos in flesh! We are *saved* from delusion and death by awakening to our essence, which is both birthless and deathless.

"He came down from heaven." He descended from his Logos/consciousness. He descended from his unmanifest eternity to his manifest presence in time. He descended from being The One into being one of the many.

"He was born of the virgin Mary." The cosmos itself was a virgin birth, begotten of nothing but the emergent being of God. In Mary, the cosmos was born a second time, a second virgin birth, the eternal itself made manifest as space/time and energy/matter.

"He was crucified under Pontius Pilate." In other words, he truly was a human person, part of history, subject to the sneering egos who crucified him by manipulating a Roman named Pontius Pilate. In this horrendous death, Jesus identified with all who suffer and die at the hands of the ignorant and the cruel. Jesus suffered capital punishment for no crime whatsoever. Jesus was a true Jew, the first of the Holocaust, killed by an insane regime incapable of recognizing his divinity. He was put to death by those who should have known better.

"He suffered death and was buried." An affirmation that he really died and his body was put back into the earth. Ashes to ashes, dust to dust. And then the third virgin birth: again, born of the tomb/womb of the Great Mother Earth.

"On the third day he rose again." Death was not victorious over life because it is not the opposite of life. Death is the opposite of birth. Life is a continuum from the eternal unmanifest through the eternal/temporal manifest. Life *IS* the ChristLogos made manifest in time. We cannot die because we *ARE* life and life is Christ and Christ is God. This above sentence is the "Good News" we call gospel: we cannot die! We all suffer "death" of the body as the form wears out and becomes its constituent organic molecules once again. But just as the heat that leaves the body at death is eternal (energy is neither created nor destroyed), we too are eternal life. We are the presence of God and cannot come to an end. Rising from death is proof that death has no final or fundamental reality. In time we have this particular life form; in death we are all of life again.

"He ascended into heaven and is seated at the right hand of the Father." The ascension of Jesus represents his realization of his essential nature as ChristLogos. He awakened from a separate egoic experience to his true experience as God's life present throughout the universe. Being seated at the right hand of the Father is a condescending and trivializing way to say that he ascended to his pre-temporal identity as a function of God, as ChristLogos, and was then present as such throughout space and time, and still is. It was precisely in that fashion that he was able to ordain St. Paul after his own death. As ChristLogos, he re-achieved omnipresence.

"He will come again to judge the living and the dead, and his kingdom will have no end." His life as ChristLogos is the glory shining forth throughout the created order. The glory of billions of galaxies containing billions of stars. The glory of Earth and her life systems of water, soil, and air. The glory of all of life, birthless and deathless, born and dying in a trillion forms. And his presence in all forms creates the judgment from within. With the guilt of living in contradiction to his life within, which is our life, there is a moment of eternal judgment, the inability to go on without emptying, sunyata, in confession. "His judgment" is our own judgment of our selves, of the false selves we build to cover our essential, our eternal and divine selves. To borrow from twelve-step recovery programs, we "hit bottom" in our attempt at living in a fake self. Then, we too rise from that "death" and "ascend" into awakening. Awakening transcends death and we live in a kingdom that has no end. Eternal life lies within our temporal forms, which in being born must die. But the kingdom of life has no end.

"We believe in the Holy Spirit." We need to believe in the Holy Spirit until we know the Holy Spirit as the life of God beneath the temporal masks we wear. When we know the Spirit, we know our life is that Spirit and we know that the cosmos itself abides in and as that same Spirit. Christian ecology is the recognition of divine life in all life forms. We treat the whole created order as manifest divinity *because it is!*

"We believe in one holy catholic and apostolic Church." The Greek words *kata holos* when joined come out as "cathalos," or Catholic. The words mean "the whole" or "according to the whole"—the whole Church and the Church of the whole. The ChristLogos contains the whole created order and is the spirit within it. The catholic Church contains and is contained by all manifestations of The One. St. John made this clear in the opening lines of his gospel (John 1:3): "Because nothing came to be except through him, all that is is him." The catholic Church, or universal church, is the church of the whole universe. And it is not just Christians!

"The communion of saints, ..." Because birth and death are opposites and because life has no opposite, when we "die" to the small, egoic self and "rise" to our actual nature in eternal life, God's life, we have access to or are in communion with all of life. All of life means past life, the present, and even future life. Past, present, future equals three times in one, which is eternal. *Com-unio* means "union with." The communion of saints is the reality we witness in so-called ancestor worship in Eastern and indigenous cultures. In the West, we prefer to call this phenomenon the intercession of the saints. The point is the same and Pope John Paul II made that clear. Life forms are born and they die, but life is eternal.

"The forgiveness of sins, ..." As the epidemic of addiction illnesses continues to gnaw at Western civilization, it becomes ever more clear that the loss of grounding in an experiential knowledge of God has much to do with the meaninglessness, the hopelessness, and the depression/despair that are its root cause and most obvious symptom. The trivialization of Christianity has much to do with this spiritual illness. As Alcoholics Anonymous has shown, a surrender (Step Three) to an experiential knowledge of God (called "consciousness contact" in Step Eleven) is a necessary prerequisite to healing or sobriety. When the addiction illness is healed, the behavioral "sin" (missing the mark) is forgiven. The deep, ontological healing erases the surface behavior. Later, in our dealing with the unitive rite of emptying, or confession, we will note that this process amounts to the erasure of karma. Karma, cause-and-effect, is one of the laws of creation and we saw earlier that laws of creation are expressions of the mind of Christ. Jesus himself pointed to karma in saying, "As you sow, so you reap; the measure you measure out is the measure measured back to you." Jesus, resurrected and ascended as ChristLogos, *IS* what is called the akashic record, or the universal database or memory of karma; karma is his to erase, to forgive, to forget. When Christ forgets the event, it is no longer present in the cosmos—it never happened! Confession in mainline Christianity has been either abandoned altogether or made silly and trivial. The whole Church needs to study the Twelve Steps of Alcoholics Anonymous and then go to confession. Two millennia of Christianity will die and third-millennium Christianity will rise from that death. The Ascension of Christ will again inform the interior spirit of Western culture. And his life in other cultures, whether called the Tao, Mind, Brahman, or whatever, will be self-evident. If "we believe in one God," who else can it be?

"And life everlasting." Life just is everlasting; it manifests God and God is everlasting. In the "giving forth" the for-giveness of "our sins," we ascend and awaken to our own immortality. Transcending death, we are free to live, we and all other life forms.

"Amen." As noted above in the Lord's Prayer, Amen is the Western equivalent of Om. It also means "this is true and I believe it"! And I do.

CHAPTER II

The Surrender Prayer and the Robing Prayer

L ate in the year 2000, I, my wife, and a dear friend began praying together. That prayer led, by Easter 2002, to the forming of the Order of Christian Mystics. We saw ourselves in service to each other and to a group of about a dozen others who showed some interest. These dozen others and we eventually referred to ourselves together as the Church of Christ the Mystic. Later, two more people joined the order. The church and the order grew quickly and powerfully and then simply ended. In all, the experience lasted about five years.

We had a liturgy of silence, a communal consecration of gifts of bread and nonalcoholic fruit of the vine. We understood that Christ in our midst, Christ in the gathering, was the consecrating priest. We each brought our own silent blessings, our consecrations, to the table, and then we shared the gifts among ourselves. The presence of God was overwhelming. We held an Easter vigil ceremony in 2002, complete with blue denim Franciscan-style robes. Here below is the prayer of consecration we used to vow into the Order of Christian Mystics. It is offered to you should you choose to take this vow of surrender. If so, you become a member, wherever you are. In a later chapter, I will explain the possible creation of a worldwide fellowship, of which, as is the case with Alcoholics Anonymous, you are a member when you say you are a member. So, here is the surrender prayer.

The Surrender Prayer of the Order of Christian Mystics

> Today, I vow my life to God, my Source,
> The Way, the Truth, and the Light.
> I promise to live in service to all creation.
> I promise to take full responsibility for my life.
> I surrender to God and will live without active
>   addiction.
> I recognize that God is present everywhere,
> and is the answer to all fear.
> The Word of God can be trusted,
> and is a place of refuge for all who seek.
> Therefore, I offer my life to the building of a new
>   culture
> through, with, and in the Order of Christian
>   Mystics.
> I take refuge in Christ Jesus.
> I take refuge in the Word.
> I take refuge in the Order of Christian Mystics.
> This day and forever. Amen.

Many have said things similar to the following: "I want to surrender, but how?" The words provide a form for your intention. The omnipresent ChristLogos is aware of that intention and honors it. The surrender should be done on one's knees; kneeling indicates and engenders humility and surrender. If, for any reason, it isn't possible to get on your knees, any position will do as long as sincerity is present. The internal disposition and not the external behavior is in the end the vital ingredient. Confucius actually used the word "sincerity" rather than enlightenment.

Robes and vestments are tricky things. The original intention behind them was to play down the individuality that gives birth to the ego-self: "If we all wear the same things, we can't compete; under this robe, we are equals before God." Presently, however, one often gets the sense that people's egos are really invested in their robes. It makes them a Franciscan or a Buddhist or a Hindu. The message becomes: "Look at me! I'm special." So, in the Order, we agreed to wear the robes only when alone or when alone with each other. We began using the following prayer every morning as a reminder of our surrender and as a sort of "mental robing." This prayer is to be said daily before entering the business of life, where we are in fact dressed like everyone else. It is a way to remember the vow we took at the moment of our surrender. It is the attitude that truly does make us different in the right way. So, here is the daily robing prayer.

The Daily Robing Prayer

I begin this day, Oh God
Calling to mind that I live
Robed in the blue of sky and ocean,
In cotton formed of soil, water,
Air, and sun.
And my belt
Grown in the fields of the Earth.
Thus clothed in Your Creation,
Surrendering all addictions,
Vowed in lifelong service
To Your whole creation,
I pray to Mary and Francis, saying,
I take refuge in Christ Jesus.
I take refuge in the Word.
I take refuge in
The Order of Christian Mystics.

Then we just go about any service work we are called by God to perform.

A word about the robe: Should you desire a robe for private meditation, the following describes the ones we used. First, it is a

Franciscan-style robe made of blue denim, 100% cotton. A hemp rope circles the waist with three knots at the two ends of the rope, one end with two knots and one end with one. These represent the three refuges: to Christ Jesus, to the Word, and to the Order. The rope represents the biosphere, the thin strip of life at the earth's surface. The blue robe above the rope represents sky and the blue below it, ocean. A grey wool or cotton shawl is worn over the shoulder and down the front in prayer-meditation. It represents clouds that create oceans and support the biosphere. We are barefoot in order to feel the earth or wear brown sandals representing the soil we walk upon and are made of. Jesus told us to pray in our closets, meaning prayer-meditation alone or in private. We only use the robe when we cannot be seen by others except for other Order members.

PART III

The Unitive Rites

A Note on the Unitive Rites

From its beginning, Christianity has had sacraments or rituals, inherited from Judaism before it. All sacraments are designed to be meeting places between humanity and God. We could see each of them as windows into the one ritual that is the universe itself. The universe ritual is the expression of God's very being in energy and matter, in space and time. Sacraments are meant to be windows into the very being of God. Sacraments that function properly allow humans to identify their own being as subsets or functions of the one being of God. This is true of unitive spirituality in its entirety and even more so with the unitive rites.

If we were to allow ourselves the right of poetic license, we could sum up much of Confucian thought in the following series of statements:

> If the individual is in order, the family will be in order.
> If the families are in order, the neighborhood will be in order.
> If the neighborhoods are in order, the town and city will be in order.
> If the towns and cities are in order, the nation will be in order.

If the nations are in order, the continent will be in order.
If the continents are in order, the planet will be in order.
If the planets are in order, the solar system will be in
order.
If the solar systems are in order, the galaxy will be in
order.
If the galaxies are in order, the universe will be in order.
If the universe is in order, humans will become third
partners with Earth and heaven.

The experience of third partnership with Earth and heaven could be called sacramental mysticism. The unitive rites seek to open individuals to their true planetary and cosmic identities. To experience one's cosmic identity is to realize one's being as an extension of the eternal in time. In saying "I and the Father are one," we are realizing our cosmic identity, our true self. *Nam myoho renge kyo* is the Buddhist equivalent of St. Paul's saying that he no longer lived but that Christ lived in him.

To know ourselves as the presence of the infinite, or the eternal, in a succession of moments in time is to know God—as our own being and as the being of all others. This God we know as our own being and identity is, for Christians, the ChristLogos, the creative dynamics of God. There is simply nothing else to know!

CHAPTER 12

The Rite of Annunciation

It is clear in the Gospels that the conception, or Annunciation, of Jesus represents the joining of eternity with time, the manifestation of divinity in the human life form. Mary's reception of the divine life within her womb resulted from her ecstatic experience of total self-surrender. Conception brings us face to face with the mystery of Incarnation. Like the birth of the universe, itself the eruption of the eternal made temporal, Annunciation/conception/incarnation represents a further spark flung from the same divine source. We, each of us, is such a spark; we, each of us, is sacramental in our Annunciation/conception/incarnation. The whole universe, Earth and life communities in their being and evolution, are implicated in every conception, whether plant, animal, or human. As noted in Chapter 5, life itself is the sacrament of Earth.

The two cells that sparked our Annunciation when joined, pre-existed that conception in our parents. The carriers of those two cells, our parents, were themselves part of an unbroken genetic sequence leading back from the present cultures to earlier culture forms, back to the primates, and to the early mammals, back through the birds, reptiles, and amphibians, back to early marine life forms in the ocean, and back to a pre-biological Earth. Earth, in turn, emerged from the solar system, the solar system from the universe, and the universe from the silence we call God. Every conception is the expression of eternity in time. Regardless of marital status, every conception is the product of the one great ritual that is the universe. There was a time in the Christian story when Mary herself was an unwed mother. Perhaps knowledge of that fact, of his mother's suffering and fear at that time, caused Jesus to refrain from condemning the woman caught in adultery. Each of us is a ritual within that larger ritual of eternity pouring into time. This all happens through the joining of DNA. If there is a word of God in matter, it is DNA.

As Christian mystics, our understanding of the sacredness of Annunciation/conception ought to be played out in our communities. Here is the first of the great feminine rites. Here is the moment when women, sparked by new life, become the meeting place of time and eternity. The dignity of this event cannot be overestimated. Neither theology alone nor mythology alone can do it justice. The depth of this truth requires the endorsement of experience, of mysticism. Without direct experience, we only know "about" Annunciation. When a woman experiences this great gift, the announcement of it should cause the community to constellate around her. A pregnant woman is the very nucleus of her community. Each community should host a public gathering around her. She is Bethlehem in our midst. It is our privilege to serve her and the divinity she carries within.

Mystical theology is a theology of silence. In silence, the Word is spoken again. In the rite of Annunciation, the Word of God, the BioLogos, is made flesh again. Now the mother will draw the water, soil, and air into herself and into the child within. From those Earth ingredients, the body is formed. As such, both mother and child become third partners with Earth and heaven.

Suggested Ritual

When the announcement of conception occurs, the community forms a meditation-praying circle around the mother. In silence, the *prayers* and good wishes are allowed to flow from the circle to its nucleus. Following fifteen to thirty minutes of this silence, the whole community applauds and shares a meal. Now the community itself is made third partners with Earth and heaven as well.

CHAPTER 13

The Rite of Nativity

Most of us are familiar with the Christmas story—Jesus born in a manger among the animals. In it, the self of the universe is understood to be incarnate as the self of this little body. Eventually, the self of that body would again become the self of the body of the universe. There is a powerful eco-unitive symbol in the Hebrew Bible, or Old Testament. Following the flood, Noah, his family, and the animals are all safe in the ark. The ark is a symbol of Earth, of the womb—a place where the whole life community is held in safety. In the manger, God as mammal is born among the other mammals. He could have chosen birth in a palace; he was, after all, in the royal line of King David. Instead, he came forth among the life forms who themselves came forth from him. Thus, the manger becomes the Ark of the New Covenant.

Nine months of dwelling beside Mary's beating heart and breathing lungs, Jesus emerges. Placed at her breast, the fourth chakra, he is restored to her breath and her heartbeat. We can imagine Jesus, like any infant, tugging greedily at Mary's breast. Perhaps standing behind him, a calf performed the same life ritual at the teat of his bovine mother. Here is the great feminine Eucharist: "Take, eat, this is my body." First ex utero comfort of each and every mammal ever born. No fussiness here, just the primal life ritual among the other life forms. The good smell of the dung of cattle, the soft breath of the animals warming the incarnate source of the universe. Mary, split open and bleeding, as Yahweh emerges in the form of an infant. Hay, blood, screams, hair, stars singing in the night, the lowing of cattle! Poor Joseph, like every man, offering his slim comfort when there is no comfort to give!

The evolving Christian mystic comes to see that every birth is a rite of nativity, that every nativity is the birth of the ChristLogos among us. That every child born of woman is an individuated form of the one God. That every child has inherited in his or her own being the supreme depth and infinite value of the whole universe process. That every birth is a micro-nativity, the most recent expression of the macro-liturgy that is the universe. Nativity, the second of the great feminine rites, is the incarnate creativity of the life community, the Earth, the galaxy, the universe, and—transcendent of them but imminent within them—the mind of God. Birth reminds us that we dwell as miracles in a universe of the miraculous. Mysticism awakens us to that fact; mysticism reveals the sacrality of all that is.

Mystics are called to break out beyond the body, or ego-self, and to realize their own self in the whole body of the universe. In doing so, we feel the millions whose bodies starve because we are those same people! When our self becomes the ChristLogos, we feel the death of other species in the ark, in the manger. We feel the horror of the millions who are not afforded safety in the womb, denied entry at the inn. This is why Christian mystics speak for life. Christian mystics speak for life, as life, because we are life! As we break through the little ego-self of "this body" we become the self of the neighborhood, the self of cities and towns, of nations, continents, Earth, the solar system, the galaxy, and the universe. Third-millennium Christianity and Christian ecology emerge from that realization. The rite of Nativity is a reaffirmation of that experiential truth.

⊚ ———————————————————————————

Suggested Ritual

As with marriages and even deaths, Annunciation and Nativity should be causes of celebration. Marital status should

never be a consideration regarding the child to come forth.
The private nativity rite is obviously the birth ritual itself.
When the woman or couple is ready, she or they should again
be circled by the meditating community. That same community should be the location of the third rite, the rite of Baptism.

CHAPTER 14

The Rite of Baptism

Nothing in the nature of hydrogen or oxygen alone could pre-pare us for the advent of water. When they come together as a compound, two volatile gases reveal properties of wetness and fluidity. These properties are totally novel with regard to their constituent atoms. Two explosive gases when wed produce the liquid that can extinguish fires. Water is the very basis of life, a miracle like no other. In its presence to us is a sequence of transformations that actually precede space/time and energy/matter. Water is a form that consciousness takes on.

I said earlier that the universe was born of the matrix (matter) of consciousness itself born of divinity. We can "see" the beginnings of H_2O in the primordial hydrogen and helium that emerged when the radiation phase of the early universe came to an end and cooled into matter. We can follow hydrogen born of energy, itself born of consciousness, through its next transformation from first-generation star, to supernova, to second-generation star, and the formation of the solar system. As the sun-planets system emerged from the proto-solar disc, we can speak of the emergent Earth. Earth went through various upheavals in its failed attempt to become a star. These led to off-gassing, and the consequent cooling and formation of clouds. From clouds came rain and the consequent hydrologic cycle of Earth. Like an old apple, the planet contracted and wrinkled and over millions of years, the basins of the rivers and seas formed in those wrinkles. Life emerged from those seas and in time green plants appeared, inhaling the early toxic atmosphere and exhaling oxygen. Oxygen was born of a living Earth.

The living human hand writing these words is part of a water-based life form. Hydrogen from the heavens and oxygen from the Earth have evolved to the point that they are able to reveal the consciousness that is their source in the writing of this. When that hand is cupped to scoop water over the head of another, the head, the hand, and the water all point back to the Trinity, their common source. Water is the extended finger of God touching us. Water is the mater-ial component of baptism, and consciousness is its spiritual component. What would baptism mean if we used polluted water? If water does reach to us from eternity, whom do we violate when we pollute? As baptized Christian mystics, what, then, is our responsibility to water?

Baptism is about identity. So much has been said about "cleansing from original sin" that we can miss the real meaning of baptism as becoming identified with and as the ChristLogos. We plunge into the water identified as "this person." We emerge as a new person, a ChristLogos-identified person. We all emerge with a new last name: Christ! We enter the water as Robert or Maryann and emerge as Robert Christ or Maryann Christ, as Jesus became Jesus Christ. Our dignity becomes experientially human—and experientially divine as was his. We awaken to our real identity!

Traditionally, baptism is Christianity's *initial* rite in that it *initiates* into the realization of our own eternity identity. The awakening from a separate ego identity to a unitive-divine identity is what the word salvation really means. Thus the question so many love: "Are you saved?" Damnation is life lived in the hell of a separative identity. To be "saved" is to awaken from that hell into the heaven of a unitive and eternal, an undying divine identity. We are baptized by heaven and earth in that hydrogen is from the heavens and oxygen is from the green plants of the Earth. As baptized citizens of heaven and Earth, we become third partners with heaven and Earth. *That* is salvation and nothing less than that!

Suggested Ritual

Clergy are not really needed for baptism; anyone can baptize, non-Christians included if need be. Certainly, clergy, being the "ordinary" ministers of Christian rites, will officiate more often than not. Parents, or the adult being baptized, should decide what is most meaningful to their baby or his or her self. Again, the community is united in concentric circles around the candidate. After a long meditation, the person presiding immerses or pours water over the candidate, saying, "I baptize you in the name of the Father, the Son, and the Holy Spirit."

Chapter 15

The Rite of Self-Surrender: Confirmation

The only true "confirmation" of legitimate spirituality is surrender. Whatever builds the ego-self, whatever inflates the "I-ness" and "me-ness," whatever supports separateness at the expense of union is false. To "claim" God for our personal Savior is to "grab," to take the kingdom by storm. Surrender renounces all claims, even to God or, more truthfully, our idea of God. We allow God instead to lay claim to us and to reveal the divine self through us. Truly, "anyone who finds his life will lose it; anyone who loses his life for his sake will find it" (Matthew 10:39). So in surrender, we lose our lives like a snake losing its skin. It is then that our deeper life is revealed—only then.

This rite can be done at any time in life and it can be repeated many times. However, it is first offered to adolescents at the time when the procreative fires emerge within them. Young people are invited to surrender their procreative powers to the governance of God. In order for that to make sense to them, they must have been taught the whole story of Christ as Logos, from whom the universe, Earth, life, and culture—and their evolving bodies—are all one divine process. Rather than threaten young people with sin, guilt, and shame, we should be teaching them the sacred wonder of their procreative powers and supporting them in appropriate use of them. Sexual behavior is neither dirty nor sinful except for those blinded by ignorance of their sacredness. Right behavior comes with the appreciation of the beauty, dignity, and responsibility toward our own ability to transmit life. Jesus did not condemn the adulteress, but he did ask all of us this question: "You who are without sin, will you be the first one to condemn?" Jesus knew that the issue was not about two mammals giving each other pleasure through touch. The issue is the exchange of the BioLogos, of DNA, which sweeps us up into the creation of life—divine life, for all life is divine. The issue is DNA. More about that in the next chapter.

Traditionally, Pentecost has been the holy day of Spirit-Fire. We are taught that on Pentecost the Holy Spirit appeared as tongues of fire over the heads of the Apostles. Hindus would explain this phenomenon as the "lighting up" of the seventh or crown chakra. This descent of the Holy Spirit from above is represented by the laying on of hands. It is the birth from above that Jesus spoke of in John 3:7: "Do not be surprised when I say: You must be born from above." Two verses earlier he said: "No one can enter the kingdom of God without being born of water and the Spirit. What is born of human is human, what is born of Spirit is spirit" (John 3:5–6). To be born from above, of Spirit, and of water, of Earth, is to become third partners with Earth and heaven. Surrender of our human nature as well as of our idea of our divine nature is to die to both ideas of ourselves. In this death, we are emptied and become the womb of God's revelation of our real nature, our divine nature. In John 12:24–25, we are told: "Unless a wheat grain falls to the earth and dies, it remains only a single grain." (Unless our ego idea of a separate self dies, it remains only an ego-self.) "But if it dies it yields a rich harvest." (If it dies, it awakes to its true, universal self as ChristLogos.) "Anyone who loves his life loses it." (If we only have this I-self, this me-self, we must lose it in death because it dies with the body; it is a product of the brain and the brain dies.) "Those who hate their life in this world will keep it for eternal life." (World does not mean life on Earth, but rather life in time, the ego-life. To hate that little life is to hate our prison in time, which robs us of our true and eternal life now.) The reason surrender works with recovery from addiction is because the addicted self is that ego-self. Its death ends the power addiction has over the body. That death leads to the awakened self, the divine self, which then claims the whole person for eternal living.

Adolescence is not the time for sexual awakening only. The larger truth of adolescence is that it is also the time of awakening of idealism, the desire to serve, and most of all, a time of dawning concern for the world. Young people believe in the future, are the future, or more accurately, the future present in which they will dwell. Surrender opens the door in them for God's will to emerge, for the mind of God to begin to speak within them. We have all heard ourselves and/or others say to the young, "You can do anything you want to do." Well intentioned, but not true. I want to be center for the Boston Celtics; at 5'6" and sixty years old, it will not happen. I can't do it. A deeper love would be expressed toward the young if we helped them to truly discover God's will for them. This is done by surrender. The "I" that supposedly "can do anything" is the small egoic self. In surrender, the ChristLogos becomes the new identity. Jesus himself told us that we would do greater things than he did. All the "good advice" about finding a place in the world leads only to a life in the world. Christian mystics seek the life of heaven on Earth, the life of eternity in time.

Returning to Hinduism for a moment: The Hindu chakra system is based in seven power centers, windows of sorts from the person within to the person outside of the body. The first of these power centers is associated with the base of the spine and the instincts. The second is associated with the genital area and with procreation. The third is at the gut, and is associated with digestion and/or assimilation. The fourth is at the heart and is understood as the seat of love and compassion. Christian iconography of the "sacred heart" illustrates this chakra: from the heart of Jesus in the sacred heart iconography emanates the love of God. The fifth chakra is located at the thyroid and is associated with the overall ecology of the body. The sixth chakra is spoken of by Jesus in Matthew 6:32 and Luke 11:34, as the single eye that fills the body with light. It is located behind the brow, between the eyebrows, and appears as a disk of light with a blue outer ring in meditation. Hindus call it the *prana,* or wisdom eye. Last, the seventh chakra, the crown, is understood as the entry point of the spirit, the ChristLogos. The seventh is not really the last, but instead the first of an infinite number of chakras that lead like an umbilical cord of light back through space/time, back over the event horizon of the beginning and into eternity, the womb of God.

It is precisely from these seven centers that we "let our light shine before all." Placing the "bushel basket" of shame and guilt over any of them consists of a direct impediment to the will of God. Well-meaning but not so brilliant "teachers" have placed those baskets over one or more of these seven candles. They feared the powers they discovered abiding in themselves, probably because there were no meaningful rites of passages in which they as adolescents got help to integrate these powers. Others, very sick others, used those dawning powers in young people for their own abusive purposes. In third-millennium Christianity, we must integrate our potential for enlightenment inherent in chakra seven. Our property for spiritual insight in chakra six. Our built-in eco-wisdom in chakra five. We must find the sacred heart within, the fourth chakra, and open it to the whole creation in love. We must learn to hear the intuitive or "gut" wisdom in the third chakra and to trust that voice. We must re-joice in the sacredness of our sexual powers in the second chakra and help our children overcome the "Christian shame peddlers," celibate or otherwise. We must understand that the first chakra is a reminder that "we are Earth-mud and to Earth-mud we shall return." Integration of all seven windows allows us to let the candles burn, the light shine forth. These seven chakras are the seven churches, seven candelabras, and seven candles in the book of Revelation. If *holos* means complete or whole, then to be holy is to be complete or whole. No more piety please; it is a false self!

In mystical experience it becomes clear that the Holy Spirit or ChristLogos is the fire of the beginning. The silence and stillness of God became active in the fires of Genesis. That same Holy Spirit, or Spirit of the Whole, is the informing intelligence of evolution and the sustaining care of God within evolution. The invisible Spirit (consciousness) is symbolized by visible fire (energy), which then evolves as matter and mind. Fire preceded matter, is at the heart of matter, is the presence of God, and "shines" in the seven chakras through our material form. Consciousness is $E = mc^2$. The power of fire was evidenced on the day of Pentecost—the Apostles, awed and aware of the presence of God within them and among them. When the tongues appeared, they could speak in their own languages, and others with different languages could understand them. Why? Because mysticism is the universal language. When I hear Lao Tzu talk of the Tao, Confucius of sincerity, Aurobindo of Brahman or *sachadinanda,* Buddha of the silent emptiness of nirvana, Jews of Yahweh, or Muslims of Allah, I hear ChristLogos. It is time for the theologians and theorists of all systems to have the courtesy to be silent and to let the mystics speak. Mystics speak from experience and not from the cognitive brain. Mystics speak from eternity and not from time. Young people must find the ONE of whom the MANY were born. In that discovery, intercultural peace, the promise and mission of the third millennium can be born. The will of God is life and peace for all.

Confirmation is surrender and surrender confirms authentic spirituality. For young people being confirmed, this experience unites them to each other, each others' cultures, the other life forms, the Earth, and the universe. Thus, they become third partners with Earth and heaven. As such, they are authorized, have the authority, to speak for and as the whole creation. That awareness ignites the fire of true prophecy. Prophecy is not the ego-gratification of what we call "praying in tongues." It is the *authority* to speak with the presence of the author, of ChristLogos, of Christ the prophet. Confirmation "confirms" the mystic and opens the heart to the fires of the prophet.

Suggested Ritual

The community forms concentric circles around the person about to be confirmed and meditates for some minutes. That person then breaks the silence by reciting on his or her knees a surrender prayer written by him or her. The spiritual leader chosen by the the person comes forward and makes the sign of the cross with oil on the person's forehead, the sixth chakra, and then lays hands on him or her over the seventh chakra and whispers "Receive the Holy Spirit." After another period of silence, the community applauds and a banquet is held in honor of the newly born mystic and prophet.

This ritual can be done for the confirmation of one person, or more than one. Each person may have a spiritual leader, or the whole group being confirmed may share a spiritual leader.

CHAPTER 16

The Rite of the Eucharist: Food

What could be more common than a shared meal? "Want to meet for lunch?" We have all heard it, said it, a thousand times. Meals hold families together. The loss of family meals, in my experience as a counselor, is one of the root causes of the disintegration of the family as a bio-spiritual and cultural institution in the United States. Regular family dining fills a need, the absence of which can never really be remedied by group counseling. Again: "if the individual is in order, the family is in order; if families are in order, the neighborhood will be in order." And so on. The shared meal provides experiential knowledge and ordering of our larger selves: the family. In a family, we learn how to create family. Otherwise we soon forget; family-making is not genetically transmitted.

Jesus left us a meal he inherited from the Jewish *shabbat*. He learned it, in other words, in his family. Bread and wine; it does not get much simpler! Bread, formed of grasses, grows by the mingling of sunlight, water, and organic compounds. As noted earlier, the formation of Jesus' body within the habitat of Mary's womb took shape in the same way. Wine, or the fruit of the vine, was and is formed in the same way. Again, sunlight is captured by plants, mingled with soil and water, and evolves as grape. In other words, the sun-planet system brings forth grass, grape, and animal life forms. The solar system is a product of the galaxy and the galaxy of the universe. When Jesus said, "Take, eat, this is my body; take, drink, this is my blood," he was speaking as the self of the universe. It is thus literally true.

"Glory be to the Father, to the Son and to the Holy Spirit, as it was in the beginning, is now and ever shall be, world without end, Amen." There really was no beginning. What we call "the beginning" was a fluctuation in the silent stillness of God, a fluctuation allowing the expression of movement and creativity. At the emergence of space/time and energy/matter there was only God; again, as it *was* in the beginning. "Was" is past tense. "Before Abraham was, I am" (John 8:58)—Jesus used the same past tense in expressing his nature as ChristLogos. Prior to the beginning God *was,* consciousness *was* and only consciousness *was.* The only stuff available for a universe to form *was* the stuff of consciousness, of God. Again, consciousness is $E = mc^2$. Energy and matter are denser forms of consciousness, of God. Again, there was no beginning; eternity fluctuated and evolved as energy, matter, and mind. There is no "divine dimension" to the universe; the universe is itself divine in its totality. To participate in communion, or Eucharist, is to participate in a special or concentrated form of divine food. It could be said that "we come together to eat God." One could ask, "If all food is a product of consciousness, then why isn't McDonald's the same as Eucharist?" Because of the divine intention expressed by Jesus as ChristLogos. He was not speaking as the carpenter's son; he was speaking as ChristLogos. Thus, a new creation came into being, a new level of bio-spiritual evolution. Jesus gave us the ability to ingest the unmanifest God in manifest bread and wine. Mytho-spiritually we read, "Let there be light, and there was light." The Gospels then add, "Let them eat light; and there was Eucharist." Christ present in the community gathered together consecrates the gifts. There is no magic in ordained priesthood; the presider merely articulates the form of words.

So, "when we eat this bread and drink this cup," whom exactly are we eating? What is food addiction? What is wine addiction? Whom are we seeking? Whom do we hunger for? I once read a Jungian commentary in which it was suggested that the widespread epidemic of eating disorders and substance dependence in Western cultures might spring from the loss of the communion banquet. What if communion, Eucharist, really is the ability to eat God? No wonder we are spiritually starved; no wonder we don't have the psychic energy, the fuel to solve our individual and collective problems. With all the foods available in America we find ourselves obese and still starving! If this seems possible to you, then come on home. We're having God for dinner!

Suggested Ritual

The gathering as always is configured in concentric circles around a simple table with a cup of wine and a plate with simple bread on it. (Use grape juice if there is even one person present recovering from substance abuse. Nowhere in the actual words of consecration in the Gospel does Jesus use the word "wine." Following the words of consecration he might mention that he will not drink wine again until after his death, but not once is "wine" used in consecration itself.) The whole gathering meditates silently and silently says a consecration prayer. Following this meditation and still in silence, the gifts are passed among those present. Then again, silence and meditation are followed by a silent departure.

The ChristLogos present in those present is the consecrating priest. In a traditional congregation, the priest/minister can still say the consecrating words out loud between the two periods of meditation. In that way, "the Word will be spoken in the silence." This is indeed the actual case for Genesis and Eucharist; from silence comes the Word.

CHAPTER 17

The Rite of Marriage: Sexual Love

All species have mating-specific behaviors and mating rituals, and humans are no exception. Because humans are cultural as well as biological beings, our mating rituals too have cultural as well as biological components. The fact that perhaps all cultures have some form of marriage ceremony underscores the universality of this truth. We seldom consider our sexual behavior at the species level. Nonetheless, it seems obvious that until we understand the deep cultural and spiritual aspect of it as a unitive dimension of the biological-procreative aspect, we will continue to witness the disintegration of the family. Why? Because families not created properly do not hold together properly. The individuals must be "in order" for the couple to be "in order." The couple must be "in order" for the family to be "in order," and so on. Ordering amounts to the unitive joining of time, the body form, and eternity, the soul. So, what, then, is our ritual and how do we enact it? Our goal of course is the well-being of human young, in utero, ex utero, and throughout their development.

If we are to succeed in this, we must discover a ritual form that is true for our biological as well as for our spiritual and cultural nature. It must be true for both natures or it cannot be true. So let us look at the behavioral ritual itself. I am suggesting that it has six archetypal stages: meeting, recognition, courtship, engagement (public announcement), communal vows, and consummation. Unitive marriage is the goal in the statement "The two shall be one." True intimacy is oneness, unity. It is the joining of our spiritual beings by becoming permeable to each other through vulnerability. If we are secure enough, safe enough with each other to become vulnerable, permeable, penetrative, we can then symbolize that permeability through joined bodies and mingled DNA. If vulnerability is not present, counseling or parting is indicated. So, the ritual behavior is the methodology of permanent union, for a unitive marriage. Let us discuss the stages.

MEETING: Many people come into and exit from our lives in a single day. Certain people among them, once in a great while, make a deep impact on us when we meet. We experience an undeniable attraction that we can neither explain nor forget. Certain looks or mannerisms of these people are profoundly pleasant to us, even euphoric. Sometimes we even see the light of consciousness surrounding them; they are beauty-full. Sometimes, we feel as though time stops and eternity can be felt in their presence. We catch a glimpse of them in the way God sees them and with the same pleasure. It is as though we have been holding our breath all our lives and can finally exhale. Both friendships and romantic love begin in this way; they are unitive. It is as though we have recognized each other, and we have!

RECOGNITION: Over time, and sometimes very quickly, this recognition deepens into something of primary importance to us. We can become preoccupied with the idea of being with this person. Other relationships and interests can become secondary or slip into unimportance. If we have a spiritual language, we talk about ourselves feeling "whole" (holos) with this person, awake or inspired. The relationship begins to take on a universal dimension. We feel that we cannot explain our experience, that no one could possibly understand. We begin to sense the oneness of God, as though our meeting somehow completes a previously incomplete universe. We talk of being "in" love, and we are.

COURTSHIP: With this recognition, courtship has begun. Courtship is a slow behavioral dance, a slow joining of souls, a sharing of spiritual cytoplasm. The interior lives of two become the interior life of one. We begin to "hear" each other's thoughts, to "feel" each other's feelings. We want more than anything else to enter into physical behaviors but if we can postpone them, the sleeping God within the two souls will awaken and become unitive in an ecstatic flow of devotion. We experience an urge to bring our love into the community, to family, to church or temple. Whatever the season of Earth, it is springtime for us!

Since the late 1960s, it is at this stage or even earlier that intercourse often takes place. In the film industry, the moment of recognition and the moment of consummation are often the same moment. Many of my clients, while grieving a failed relationship, have admitted that they knew deep in their soul that the relationship failed at this point, at the advent of sexual behavior. They describe a "sinking feeling," a spiritual pain that they then tried to deny. There are reasons for this. The exchange of DNA (the BioLogos) activates a triune relationship between the two people and God. The soul, requiring meaningful commitment in order to be vulnerable and allow permeability, withdraws. That withdrawal is the sinking feeling; it is spiritual pain. If the soul withdraws, the body loses interest because the unitive conditions are no longer present. What might have been a unitive marriage becomes a painful marriage. We can insist and persist on the behavior, but the true bonding has been impaired if not destroyed.

Who knows why the soul will refuse to bond to another without the fact of commitment? It is like asking why is there gravity? Or why is water wet? These are just the way the ChristLogos orders creation from within. Truly holy orders! Standing on the edge of a cliff, one can either accept the "truth" of gravity or not. We are all free to jump. I would suggest that the reason the soul pulls back without commitment is that unless a properly bonded (ordered) family is in place, the emergence of another human soul/child is not safe or is at least unstable. At the species level, we marry in order to create the optimum physical and spiritual habitat to receive human young. Does that mean that sex is only for procreation? No! It means that DNA exchange is about procreation. Procreation is not just about "this man" and "this woman." A divine third is present in the joined DNA and its new Annunciation. A family is the committed, the bonded biological-spiritual context selected through evolution and therefore by God and nature for the raising of human young.

Touching and the play of love does not include this genetic/divine exchange. We are of course assuming age appropriateness and mutual consent. All mammals are givers and receivers of physical pleasure. We as a species are both mammals and primates. Many ask why divine evolution would design us in this way, only to rule out pleasure exchange as immoral. The danger of sexual play is that it can lead to the exchange of DNA but it does not necessarily need to do so. Human intercourse, the complete joining of bodies and souls in sexual unity, includes the possibility of the transmission of life. Life is eternal; life is divine; life is God's presence; life is holy. Kissing and touching do not necessitate the actual union of DNA with DNA (the Word in flesh). The black-and-white thinking of no sexual contact prior to matrimony can still be encouraged and supported. Still, it lacks meaning to most Westerners these days and probably always has. However, joined DNA (Definitely Not Advised), treating superficially the union of man, woman, and God as well as the newly conceived offspring, often leads to personal tragedy. And, the jump made from meeting to recognition to courtship to consummation can and often does abort the bonding of the souls who otherwise truly do love one another. It prevents man and woman from becoming one, from becoming third partners with Earth and heaven. It introduces disorders into the individual, into families or would-be families, into neighborhoods or towns. Sometimes, it brings discord to entire nations. We cannot treat lightly the evolution of life. When we do so, we do so at our own peril.

Courtship is also the period when we come to know each other in depth and develop the skills necessary to name and resolve our differences. Each of us is highly differentiated. Each of us has infinite interior depth. Each of us is in communion with all that is. If we avoid the developmental work necessary to explore differences and subjectivities, we never come to the unitive oneness that provides communion. Still, the differences are inherent in each of us; we really are unique. A few years into marriage and more than half fail, at least in the United States. Collectively, we have created a nation of semi-orphans. If it didn't require a man and a woman to be present and to support the healthy growth of human young, it would not require a seed and an egg to conceive them. We need not argue with religion or secular ideologies; we need only to live in the simplicity of unitive truth.

ENGAGEMENT: Engagement is the public announcement of the intention to pair-bond. The community is given notice that the intentions of these two people are now deepening toward the desire to be together "until death do they part." The diamond, most durable of all stones, is the usual symbol of this intention. It is not yet the unbroken oneness of the wedding band, but it signifies a durable commitment. All other potential suitors have this last opportunity to make their bids. Following this time, vows and consummation will take place and the new human family biologically—and spiritually—unitive will be formed as the "nest," the context for human evolution.

COMMUNAL VOWS: All cultures that I am aware of possess sacred rituals that surround this stage of pair-bonding. "Culture" is the collective spirituality of a group. Primate troupes have actual cultures, ways of doing things as a group. Early human culture constellated around a holy man or woman, a shaman or shamaness. Later, Neolithic cultures saw the emergence of matrifocal (Great-Mother) rituals and belief. With the emergence of the great religious cultures East and West, the patrifocal (Great-Father) religions emerged. Presently, with the unitive confluence of global cultures, we find ourselves confused, chaotic. Third-millennium Christianity can provide a model for reassimilation, for the reawakening of a new clarity. Our vows need to reflect this new clarity, this reawakening, this renaissance. Our marriage rite must bring together not only the couple, but the whole life community, the planet, and the stars. The presence of God within the whole community, the presence of the ChristLogos, consecrates the union of the two lovers as they pledge loyalty to each other, to the community, to the universe, and to God. The two people vow and the community consecrates. Are they married? Not quite!

CONSUMMATION: The human mating ritual is only complete when DNA is exchanged in sexual union. A single cell from the male and one from the female will become one if the circumstances are correct within the habitat of the woman's womb. Openness between the two people will be profound and mysterious at this point. Union is now complete—a union that creates and imbeds the future. Problems, perhaps many problems, will emerge over the years to come. From time to time we are all attracted to others and might love several of them along the way. However, if the bonding is allowed to progress, the union will survive the heat of time, testing, mistakes, failures, and even outright betrayals. Done right, what is unitive in God no human will be able to undo. Sadly, in the Western world, our vows have almost become a mockery, a form of words empty of meaning. To recreate our culture, we must appreciate again the sacredness of marriage, of childbirth, of a shared life. We must once again bring our actions in accord with our deepest beliefs in this regard. Joined in love, we become one with each other, the life community, Earth, the universe, and God. Again, we become third partners with Earth and heaven.

◎ ───────────────────────────────

Suggested Ritual

The community is gathered as always in concentric circles. Following meditation, the rite of Communion is shared with the couple at the center with the gifts. Following the communion, the couple stands and takes the vows to one another. A brief meditation follows and then applause. As is customary, a reception follows and during that banquet the couple steps away.

When alone, the couple remembers the sacred dimension of what they are about to do. On the altar of the bed, they take their full measure of pleasure in each other. A human family may or may not be born and begin its evolution. In either case, the human mating ritual is complete.

CHAPTER 18

The Rite of Anointing

I mentioned earlier that the planet Earth is actually a series of envelopes, most dense at her core, least dense in the upper atmosphere. The envelope of life is called the biosphere, the sphere of life wrapped around the Earth's surface. All of life is eating itself, eating a blend or a mingling of organic compounds, water, and energy from the sun. In this sense, life as a whole is the child born of the marriage of Earth and sun. All green plants, called by science autotrophes or "self-feeders," are the method by which Earth captures solar energy and makes it available to the other life forms, heterotrophes or "other eaters." Green plants make food energy available to all animal life forms. The primary heterotrophes, the cattle, eat the plants. The carnivores eat the cattle and the plants and are thus called secondary heterotrophes. Omnivores such as humans eat from the whole banquet! The detrivores, the biospheric "undertakers," break down non-living forms, release their energy, and allow them to return to Earth as compost, organic compounds that will support the growth of new life forms. Birth, growth, death, decay, rebirth—the fundamental pattern of the whole life community. The use of vegetable oil in anointing rituals draws on this deep wisdom inherent in the green plants.

We seldom think much about it, but the oil of anointing, called chrism, is actually perfumed vegetable oil. The green plants also provide the bread and grapes, which become communion. They provide the very oxygen we breathe, not to mention all the fossil fuels that drive our economies. It is interesting to consider the fact that the sacredness of plants is evoked by us in their ritual use. Certainly they were sacred before we utilized them. It is we who are to awaken to their sacrality by drawing them "up" into our ritual use. They too have a history reaching back through biological, geological, and cosmological history. They too open backwards and merge with the mystery of God. They too have their source in pre-time and pre-space. I touched on this wonder, this miracle, in Chapter 16, on the rite of the Eucharist, or shared food. It is no less wonderful, no less miraculous here.

Vegetable oil, pressed from the bodies of the green plants, contains in concentrated form the ChristLogos. We are calling on that reality when we use oils to sign or anoint someone with healing. The Greek word *christus* means anointing. In their own eternal presence, the green plants provide life-food, life for every living thing. It makes sense that we would use them in our healing. To recognize (re-cognize) the presence of the whole creation is to recognize the presence of God in the oil. To bless the oil is not to change anything in the substance or make-up of the oil itself. This is not magic! Rather, blessings should serve to change our orientation to the oil, quickening our awareness of the presence of God in the green plants and in the whole life community. Christian mystics speak for the green plants because we owe our existence to them. They were selected by divine evolution to be the basic providers of the breath of life for all that lives.

In blessing another with oil, we reveal another primary human need: touch. Touch connects us, grounds us, makes us community (*comm* = with; *unio* = one). It is comforting, protective, and deeply nurturing. It was in touching Jesus and being touched by him that people were healed. Practices such as "laying on of hands" and "anointing" recognize the sacredness of touch as a function of God's desire to comfort, protect, heal, and nurture us. In anointing, the green plants are the medium through which we open ourselves to be touched by God and to be healed. The unitive rites are meeting places between God and humans. God and the Earth joined in the green plants to offer us healing and life. The chrism could be called "the prayer of photosynthesis." Through anointing, we become third partners with Earth and heaven and, in that partnership, find our healing.

Suggested Ritual

Most denominations have a form or ritual of anointing. In Christ the Mystic, the post-denominational order, we suggest that persons trusted and loved by the anointed administer the oil. Parents, friends, and siblings are more likely to allow the anointed to feel calm and comfortable. As always, the rite should arise out of and descend into meditation. The person anointing should sign the anointed with the oil at the crescendo of this rising and descending meditation. The simple words "I anoint you in the name of Christ for healing and for peace" are enough.

CHAPTER 19

The Rite of Confession:
Crucifixion and Regeneration

As mentioned several times, *sunyata* is a Buddhist term often translated as "void" or other similar meanings. Buddhist Maseo Abe translates it as "emptying," and compares it to St. Paul's statement of Christ that he "emptied himself, becoming as human beings are" (Philippians 2:8). Christianity has long had a means or methodology for emptying. It has been called the rite of Confession, or Reconciliation. It is a much ignored and in my opinion deeply misunderstood dynamic of Christian spirituality. Its absence recently is linked to the rise of psychology, talk therapy, and the confessional steps of Twelve Step programs. As Christian mystics, this profound and mysterious rite of the soul needs rediscovery. How do we crucify the ego-self? How do we empty the tomb in order to allow the Christ-self to rise from the dead? The answer is confession.

Confession, or emptying, is the way in which we repeat Jesus' descent among the dead, mentioned in the Apostles' Creed. In this case, we descend among our own dead—our denial, repressed guilt, shame, remorse, resentment, and fear. When we deny and repress, we introject those denied contents deep within ourselves. They are pressed and then re-pressed inward, disturbing the soul's ability to function naturally. The soul, our essential self, becomes buried beneath this mound of denied psychic trash. Our inner experience of resonance with this trash often causes us to suspect that we ourselves are the trash! We become entombed in this inner landfill. The result is the nearly ubiquitous lack of self-esteem we counselors hear about from client after client.

In order to cover up what we fear others will see in us, we create a mask, a false self. The Christian false self can be seen in the goody-goody, squeaky-clean person-in-miniature, praising the Lord and easily shocked at the behavior of others, judging and condemning. Identified with the denied inner content, subverting our energies to building and maintaining the false self, we shrink into a diminished mockery of what Jesus hoped his disciples would be. Groups of individual false selves create collective false selves; this is sadly what we see all about us in the major vehicles of Christianity: Catholic, Orthodox, Protestant, and Evangelical/Fundamentalist. If we are to become third-millennium Christians, if we are to be a wellspring of eternal life, we must uncap the inner well, roll the stone away from the inner tomb. We must empty ourselves in order to awaken.

First, we must come out of denial about who we have been and what we have done. In Twelve Step programs, Step One calls for an admission of powerlessness, a breaking of ego control. Next we need to admit to someone else everything we have denied and all that we have run from and tried to hide from others. We must descend into the interior hell to rescue the sleeping soul from her burial. Done deeply and consistently, the soul awakens from her burial and rises from her sleep. The mask or false self is no longer needed because the soul is no longer in hiding. The death of the mask is the crucifixion of the separate, and separated, self. We are once again who we truly are, and are once again in direct experiential relationship with God. We recall that we are the ChristLogos in this particular form that we might inhabit at present. Is it that simple? Yes, it is that simple. However, simple is not a synonym for easy. Nothing is more difficult than to face and admit all our feelings and pain to another and to God. But this is what is actually called for in James 5:16. We are called to confess our sins to one another.

There is a Judeo-Christian linkage here with the Hebrew day of atonement (at-one-ment) called Yom Kippur. The idea behind Yom Kippur is a self-admission of failings, a public admission of the same, and a making of reparation to injured parties in order to be at-oned with them again. The idea is profoundly unitive. Sadly, the sense I get from most of the Jews I know is that the intended depth of this process is no longer understood or practiced. What is needed is a Buddheo-Christian linkage of the idea of no-self with crucifixion/confession.

Buddhists speak of a condition they call "no-self." It is easy to misunderstand the meaning of no-self. When we make the mask or false self obsolete by emptying (sunyata), the real self, the soul, becomes present and vibrant again. The soul made of God becomes a window again, a venue for divine light. When the soul is alive and functioning, the self we truly are once again manifests the spirit of God. Buddhists acknowledge the presence of Mind throughout the universe. No-self really means no false self. Mind can be understood by Christians as ChristLogos. Call it Mind, call it Logos, call it Spirit—it is the presence of the one in the many. In emptying and destructuring the false self, we become local venues of a nonlocal omnipresence. We know that we and the Father are one, we know that the egoic self no longer lives but that Mind lives in us. For "crucified Christians," those emptied and redeemed from the egoic self, no-self is better understood as "true self," a cleansed window of the many through which the light of the one God may shine into the world. Crucifixion of a dead, brittle self leads to regeneration of a supple, vibrant reborn soul. To speak of being a reborn Christian without this crucifixion is to speak from the false self that prevents the very rebirth we claim. Awakened from her sleep of separation, the soul remembers her union with all of life, the whole planet, solar system, and galaxy, and becomes wed again to Earth and to heaven. The idea of crucifying a brittle and wornout false self so that the supple truth of the soul can be regained is what Jesus was pointing to in Mark 2:22, when he talked about old and new wineskins.

Suggested Ritual

The best guides for the written inventory that precedes the actual confession come out of the Twelve Step community. And the best of these is available through a particular kind of Alcoholics Anonymous meeting called the Big Book Step Study Process. Being an alcoholic or addict is not central to these meetings. Nonaddicts and nonalcoholics can get a sponsor or guide through the written inventory process. I myself did the process and it took me sixteen months for the written part and thirty-three hours for the actual confession, or Step Five. I did eleven sessions of three hours each. Once the written inventory, or Step Four, is complete, you should begin the spoken portion.

It is of supreme importance to work with the right person. Ordination or licensure can help because of underscoring confidentiality. However, only someone who "knows the terrain" can guide properly. Each person must find the right partner. Once this is done, the partners should meditate together and then begin the confession. Another meditation should follow and then a short prayer to conclude. The spoken confession should arise out of silence. The final prayer should also arise out of silence. If the community is open to it, a meditation together after completion should conclude with a communal applause or celebration and a recognition that "the lost one has been found; the dead one is once again alive."

CHAPTER 20

The Rite of Death and Resurrection

Each of us entered incarnation at the moment of our conception, or Annunciation. Each of us passed through the portal of our mother's birth canal in Nativity. Each of us is also destined for a final passage through the gate of time to be born once again into eternity. Death is the portal, the opposite pole of birth, and resurrection is the reawakening of life into eternity. The same intersection of eternity and time that led to conception is mirrored in the intersection of time with eternity. There is no conflict between resurrection and reincarnation for those who really understand either or both. Jesus appeared bodily following his resurrection; he was once again incarnate, re-incarnate.

We learn in high school science that energy is neither created nor destroyed; it only changes form. Since Einstein, we have known that matter is a condensed form of energy. What we are not often taught is that energy itself is a condensed form of consciousness. What I am calling consciousness is what Christians call Spirit, Buddhists call Mind, and Taoists call Tao. Consciousness is the being of God flowing over the horizon of eternity into time. Entering time, consciousness condenses into energy, and then energy into matter. We are, each of us, forms of consciousness become energy become matter. Each of us is a function of the universe and the universe is a function of God. In death, the body quickly loses its warmth, its life energy. The material form of the body begins to break down, releasing the remaining energy into the surrounding ambient environment or else through digestion by detrivores. The remaining "dust" of organic compounds rejoins the flux of the planet. "Dust to dust, ashes to ashes" we hear on Ash Wednesday. It is true that our bodies are dust and they do indeed return to dust. But as energy, we remain part of the overall flux of the universe. If energy is a concentrated form of consciousness, then we live on as that. "That thou art" say the Hindus as an attempt to name the un-nameable.

Resurrection is a fundamental truth of the universe and therefore the fundamental truth of Christianity. There is an evolution that takes place, capable of leading us to realizing our resurrection, even prior to death. Jesus showed us his Resurrection body in an event called the Transfiguration. It appears in Matthew 17:1–8, in Mark 9:2–8, and in Luke 9:28–36. He opened himself "beneath" the energy/matter of his form and made consciousness visible to those present. What then are the stages? In conception, or Annunciation, we are literally in a mater-ial environment. In utero, we are a material form within a material form, gathering material from the outside habitat, drawing it inward in order to grow. The second half of this "form within a form" is that we are also a soul within a soul. We are in a unitive state, though not in the same way as we experience it in the fully awakened or enlightened state. Same consciousness, same matter, same energy in a pre-transcendent state as opposed to a post-transcendent state. In birth, we emerge in the light of the sun as this person, this form, and are given a name. Good parenting amounts to looking within the form day by day and welcoming the universal soul within to come forward in safety. My teacher, Thomas Berry, once told me that "the baby's smile is the primary mode of universe functioning." When the baby smiles, the whole universe comes to light.

One can read any of several developmental psychologists to follow the developmental sequence as the form of the child begins to awaken to its own infinite interiority, its soul. Picture a ten-story building. Looking out from the ground floor, we see the world in a limited way—a local driveway perhaps, a parked car, dumpsters, and so on. Three stories up, we are looking at the same world, but now we see beyond the neighborhood and perhaps some distant mountains. From the sixth floor, we see beyond the city we are in and perhaps the outline of distant cities. From the ninth floor, we see to the horizon. From the rooftop, we can realize that we are embedded in the world we are looking at, that we are the same world looking at itself through us. Looking up, we can now see the sun, moon, and stars. We begin to sense that the space between the stars and the space between the atoms that make up our forms is the same space—that we are one with or a function of the whole. We begin to feel our own soul as the soul of things—that we are an expression of the whole and that others are as well. We come to understand that we have experienced our soul.

Next, we might ask ourselves what soul is, what is the "stuff" that is soul? We begin to search for answers by reading the Gospels, the sutras, the Tao Te Ching, the Bhagavad Gita. And in time we find that the stuff of soul is the stuff of consciousness. On the heels of that we come to see that the ChristLogos is that consciousness and that our soul is that consciousness and that our souls are ChristLogos, and therefore we cannot die! We have realized the Resurrection body prior to dying and we are free. We also see that the same stuff of consciousness is the interior life of the soul of all others and we are at one with them.

Anyone truly on his or her way to death/resurrection must appear for a time as the "man of sorrows." That stage in Jesus' life was called by some the "fool who gave everything for truth." Everyone around the man of sorrows appears "bright" while he appears "dim." Many smile "knowingly" at the man of sorrows as he agonizes in transformation. Like the caterpillar who disintegrates into a genetic soup prior to rising to a new life, the man of sorrows seems dis-integrated as he reaches for a transcendent integration. At the time, it feels like insanity until one truly arrives in sanity. True sanity is the death of the egoic self, a product of seeing oneself as a separate body, a separate life form, and an awakening to a body and self that are the universe itself, the expressed mystery that preceded it. There is no such thing as a time before time. However, there is eternity from which time is born. Eternity is the mother of time.

The portals from eternity into time and from time into eternity are presided over by the female. Jesus, born between the spread legs of a woman, nursed and bathed by a woman, was also prepared for the tomb by women. When the tomb became a womb on Easter Sunday, it was women who first realized the truth of it all. Women were midwives to the Resurrection. The three phases of the feminine could be called first, Mary, second, Earth, and third, Cosmos. The three phases of the masculine could be called first, Jesus, second, Spiritus Mundi, and third, ChristLogos. Men and women are both. Death and Resurrection are not to be avoided or covered up. Death and Resurrection are the most obvious privileges and trustworthy destiny of the Christian mystic.

◎ ————————————————————————

Suggested Ritual

To the extent possible, the dead body should be ministered to by women. One would hope for a new profession of Christian undertakers dominated by women in the way that massage therapy and nursing are. The public dimension of the wake or funeral will of course be done according to the tradition of whatever denomination the person belongs to. Post-denominational funerals will again be largely meditational, a deep contemplation on the departed spirit. Burial or cremation should follow.

PART IV

Selected Essays on Unitive Spirituality and Separative Impediments

CHAPTER 21

The Biocese versus the Diocese:
A Unitive Approach to Ecclesial Structures

What then of the Christian institution in its larger structures? How could a new and more unitive global church shape itself into administrative units? As the title of this brief essay suggests, I am suggesting a shift from the diocese to the biocese. This is not simply a semantic game. Provided with a simple understanding of a movement called "bioregionalism," the reader will soon better understand what this is all about.

Bioregionalism was a briefly lived subset of the ecological movement of the 1980s. It was based on sound scientific bio-ecological principles. I explained elsewhere that the self-organizing drive in evolution at its cosmic, planetary, biological, and cultural levels is the autopoeic (*auto* = self; *poeic* = making) structuring of reality by the presence of the ChristLogos. What the native peoples call Grandfather or Grandmother, I am calling ChristLogos. Bioregionalism is the recognition that various regions of life have their own ecosystems, species of flora and fauna, and their own mystique that becomes translated in human culture into spiritual symbolisms. For instance, the bioregional map of the continental United States, if overlaid by a map of the Native American tribes, would be almost perfectly congruent. The tribal peoples utilized the living symbols of the life forms they found around themselves to express their experience of the mystique of "this place." So, in truth, the face of God in "one place," while part of the one mystique, would nonetheless bear different features from the face of God in another place. Why? Because the creatures that co-habitated with the tribal people in these different places were different according to the ecological realities in which they found themselves.

The answer, then, to a question such as "What is a bioregion?" is a very simple one. A bioregion is a region of life! It is obvious that a desert bioregion would have very different life forms and expression of the one mystique than, say, a high-altitude mountain region. Equally clear is the difference between a forest region of life and a shore region of life. Again, a pond or lake bioregion would be different from a river bioregion. Wherever two bioregions overlap, there is created another bioregion called an *ecotome*. An ecotome is a distinct ecosystem that contains some of the species of one bioregion and some of the other, plus other life forms unique to that particular ecosystem. So the concept of bioregion is very simple.

Traditionally, the Christian church has divided itself along somewhat arbitrary boundaries derived from the political organization of the Roman Empire. The diocese is a simple geographical area articulated by human convenience rather than by natural expression of the one mystique that in this book we are referring to as the ChristLogos. The creation of a biocese would be an action taken on the part of Christianity generally, affirming the mind of the creator as it is expressed in the created order. It would be a behavioral affirmation of our belief in "one God, the Father the Almighty, the maker of heaven and Earth." It would recognize inherently that the will of God, which in the Lord's Prayer we have surrendered our will to, is best expressed in the natural order as it is. The biocese could be very simply created by a change in telephone lists and by naming, for instance, the Northeast Bioregion, which would include the forests of New England and eastern Canada. What this would do is allow the Christian establishment to get out in front of ecological thinking rather than most always being reactive to it. It would establish some sense of leadership in the recognition that all of life is divine life and that divine life expresses itself according to divine Mind, and that divine Mind is the ChristLogos among us, in our midst, and in the being and functioning of the life community surrounding us at the local level.

By creating an identity for Christians that is grounded in the natural order in the way it was for the tribal peoples, we would be building into our worship and administration an acknowledgment of and friendliness toward the other creatures in our midst. Local Christianities, subsets of The One Christianity, in the same way that local bioregions are subsets of the continental life community, could establish an Earth-imbedded symbol system that could create for our children a deep orientation to the life forms around them and a sense of place with its subsequent feelings of security. Ecopsychology tells us that rootedness to the local context and life forms produces a security and feeling of depth in the individual. In Christian ecology, this sense of depth opens backward as the ChristLogos through cultural history, biological history, geological history, galactic history, and cosmic history, and opens outward to the very presence of God out of whom we have all emerged.

CHAPTER 22

We Are All Jews:
A Unitive View of Abrahamic Religions

As obvious as it is, we seldom consider the fact publicly that Jesus was not a Christian. Jesus was a Jew. A renegade rabbi, yes, but a rabbi, a Jew. There is mounting evidence in archaeology that Jesus might well have studied in India. In considering that the historical Jesus was missing from the Gospels from the age of about thirteen until age thirty, it just makes sense that, like any other young spiritual genius, he would have followed trade routes from the Middle East to India. This might even have been arranged years before by the Hindu and Zoroastrian (and possibly Buddhist) "wise men" who journeyed to Bethlehem at his birth. If he did study with Hindus, Buddhists, and others, this would explain why he was such a different kind of Jew upon his return from the East. The changes in him, making him a heretical rabbi to this day, caused him to be put to death.

Christians, then, might be more aptly named Christian Jews or even Buddheo-Christian Jews. If Jesus was a Jew, and I am his follower, then I too am a Jew. If Jesus and Peter were Jews, then the pope is a Jew. If I am a Jew, then I can trace my spiritual heritage to Abraham. This is also true of all Muslims, making Muslims, Jews, and Christians one tradition in the sense that Hindu-Buddhism is a tradition or Taoist-Confucianism is a tradition. Brothers do not rob each other of resources at gunpoint. Brothers do not desecrate each other's house. Brothers do not bomb each other's neighborhood, whether from concealed explosives or from the air. Third-millennium Christians are called to listen to Islam and Judaism, called to study the Qur'an and the Hebrew Bible in order to resolve differences and the resultant rage.

Taking the Christian institution as a whole, we see four major vehicles. Number one is Roman Catholic; number two, Greek and Russian Orthodox; number three, Reformation *Protes*tantism; and number four, evangelical/fundamentalist Christianity. A fifth and unitive vehicle might be called post-denominational or mystical Christianity. The Catholic and Orthodox are really one tradition, separated only due to historical arrogance on both sides. We could call that tradition the Petrine tradition, the tradition of Peter. The Protestant/evangelical/fundamentalist is also one tradition; it all emerges from the Reformation. We could call it the Pauline tradition, the tradition of Paul. Mainline Christianity is split between Peter and Paul. What about Christ? Post-denominational Christianity returns to the scriptural verse, "In the beginning was the Word."

Paul too was a Jew, a rabbi. His claim of apostleship, or ordination directly by the ascended Jesus, was experiential and not associated with the traditional laying on of hands. But while Catholics and Orthodox argue century after century about theological minutia, their symbolic depth in both cases has more in common with Judaism than with Reformation Protestantism or evangelical/fundamentalism. As all four major vehicles of Christianity begin their third millennium of pettiness and squabbling, one wonders if the rabbi-guru-staretz★ of the Gospels has anything in common with any of them other than the story itself! Transcendence by way of ascendance reveals the shallow pettiness of all of them—exterior false self arguing with exterior false self! Again, third-millennium Christians, mystics, must return to the ChristLogos, the interior sentience of their lives and of all that lives. We must say with John the Evangelist, "In the beginning was the Word." We must begin again.

★Staretz is an ancient Eastern Christian word for guru.

Catholics attempt the perfect dogma, the airtight argument. Orthodox seem to defend anachronistic cultural practices of religious formalism. Reformation and evangelical/fundamentalist Protestants continue to nuance the Pauline view of Jesus in culture. Meanwhile, it seems that the mystics, those who truly do resemble the Christian mission, are silenced, held in suspicion; this has indeed been my own experience.

It is clear in reading the Gospels that Jesus dismissed the obsession with dogma. He also rejected the slavish reliance on human tradition, cultural exclusivity, and the externals of religion. Paul's statement that we must "put on Christ" almost perfectly contradicts Jesus' admonition to "cleanse the inside of the cup." Jesus talked from the inside out, in other words, about emptying and then evolving from within. I am not dismissing the four vehicles of Christian institutions as valueless, but they seem to have become unduly focused on the exterior/cognitive while often avoiding the sentient/experiential. Rather, I am asking whether any of them represent the depth of transformation called for in the face of the horror of crucifixion and resurrection.

Lacking functional methodologies for supporting in-depth transformation, the true seeker finds him- or herself facing four false-self Christianities. All false selves lack permeability and impair intimacy. In the Catholic instance, the false self is the need to be right even to the point of mass atrocities such as during the Inquisition. The false self of Orthodoxy is the mistaken emphasis on the Greco-Russianness rather than the Christianness of their traditions. The false self in Protestantism is in the lack of real protest and in their willingness to amputate whole limbs of Christianity while "putting on Christ" and building the external goody-goodyness that so disgusted Jesus himself. The false self in evangelical/fundamentalism is the power-driven fury of insisting upon literalism in a book of contradictions. The call for scripture only (sola scripture) is an idea that is itself non-scriptural! Jesus tells us not to resist evil, while James tells us with equal clarity to resist evil. Common to all four false selves is inflation and egotism.

Why? Because they lack true emptiness. They have not cleansed the cup. Lacking emptiness, the ChristLogos cannot be a "well-spring unto eternal life." Lacking the ChristLogos, they lack unity, are not unitive. What is left of Christ-ianity when Christ is no longer present? What is left is Paul.

Modern Christian mysticism, third-millennium Christianity, is the resurrection of Christ again and in our midst. It calls for a pruning back to the root of the vine. It calls for an experiential oneness among the four vehicles, expressed from within them by the one God. It also calls for a unitive approach to the other religions of the world. We are becoming one technologically, economically, and ecologically. Ecology makes it especially clear that we abide as a single species amidst the other species in a unitive and shared experience of soil, water, air, and light. Intracultural and intercultural violence with regard to the nature of God is an abomination. War about scripture is collective sin, a crime against the monotheistic God used to justify the warring ideas. He does have other sheep! They are not of one special fold! If there is ever to be "one fold," Christians are called upon to expand the meaning of the term. Other sheep and other folds must be embraced and sincerely valued rather than being tortured into a forced sameness. Economic torture is just as real as any other form of torture. It might create assent, but it never creates consent!

The false self of Christianity must be crucified. This can only be done by emptying (sunyata) the historical well of Christian tradition. Pope John Paul II began this process by acknowledging the mistreatment of Galileo and others. Attempts to cover the flagrant abuses of history, personal or collective, will prevent the resurrection of Christianity in culture. The false self is always a cover-up. To uncover the real self of Christians individually and collectively is to make the presence of Christ real, apparent throughout the planet not only in the love Christians have for each other, but also in the love for the other sheep of other folds, toward the animals and plants, the life systems of soil, air, water, and light, and toward the whole created order, the body of a living and loving God. To uncover the real self of Christianity is to uncover the living ChristLogos and his kingdom in our midst. The Good Friday, the Golgotha, of our crucified and empty selves will precede an Easter rising of third-millennium Christianity. Third-millennium Christianity will be the leaven of a new culture and a new Earth. Third-millennium Christianity will not be the Christianity of Peter or Paul, but of Christ.

CHAPTER 23

Third-Millennium Prophecy:
The Unitive Prophet

True prophets can be irritating people. Like Bob Dylan and Martin Luther King, Jr. in the sixties, they are always making us remember things we would rather forget. They force us to notice things we would prefer to ignore. They are almost always "a bit too much," "a little over the top," and "a little too intense." They speak "outside the envelope," almost always demanding more of us than we want to demand of ourselves. They call us deeper into truth, deeper than we often really want to go, perhaps even deeper than they themselves want to go! They cast light into the shadows of the skotosphere, the sphere of shadows. They seem able to read our real selves, to name our weaknesses and demand that we acknowledge more and become more. We often feel scolded by them, as though they were speaking for God, or as God's anger incarnate. We want to tell them to "tone it down," to "come off the soapbox," to "take a closer look at themselves." Occasionally, we just want to scream "Shut up!" but we go on listening. Jesus of Nazareth was a true prophet in the tradition of the Hebrew prophets. Jesus of Nazareth was a mystic who realized his ChristLogos nature, his divine nature, fused with his human nature.

And then there are safe prophets, also called false prophets. Safe prophets are charismatically powerful people with whom we already agree. The causes they champion might arouse us to remember our own beliefs. They make us conscious of those beliefs and they spur us on in expressing them; they "get out the vote." If one considered him- or herself to be a liberal overall, then safe prophets might be eco-gurus, feminists, pro-choice advocates, gay rights advocates, and so on. If our core values are liberal anyway, such prophets do not threaten us beyond those beliefs. Their passion awakens us to what we already hold to be true. They do not really threaten us; they are safe.

For those of us who are conservative by nature, those advocating issues from "the right" will awaken us to what we already believe. Anti-ecological types, anti-feminists, anti–abortion rights, and anti-gay advocates speak to a more "moral," a more traditional approach to these issues. They call out passionately against big government, against crime, and, in that context, for capital punishment. Those who long for "simpler times," whether real or imaginary, will naturally awaken to the voice of such prophets. They provide leadership in support of these issues and keep them in the public eye. But assuming that we already agree about such issues, we will not be threatened when they are brought into our awareness and kept there. We might welcome the support we feel for our already-formed beliefs. If we agree already, we might be energized and not threatened; for us, these too would be safe prophets.

It is interesting to consider that all of these positions, left and right, have a moral basis in the prophetic tradition of the Hebrew prophets, including Jesus of Nazareth. From the left, there is the moral call to ecological balance, to the sacredness of the created order. From the right, the call is to use the planet for the betterment of humanity. From the right, there is a call for women to provide homes for humanity, to be concerned for children, to recreate and nourish the fundamental building blocks of all societies. From the left, the call is for equal opportunity for women to express their own giftedness in the other realms of life—political, economic, educational—with equal rights and equal pay guaranteed. From the left, the support for "choice" is grounded in the above liberty, to free women from the limitations of the domestic environment and the domination of men and/or government in very private decisions. From the right, anti-abortion activists recognize the lack of "choice" for the pre-born; they are defending the rights of the most vulnerable class of human life. Liberals call for greater "liberty." Conservatives call for "conservation" of tradition and values. Both liberal and conservative philosophies and political underpinnings come from a prophetic tradition that calls for justice, equality, and equal responsibility. They are, in fact, halves of a greater whole, a unitive whole. "Half-truth" is the real meaning of the word *heresy*. Both liberal and conservative moralities are half-truths, and in that sense, equally heretical!

The true prophet, the unitive prophet, would threaten everyone involved by reuniting the half-truths into a unitive whole. The unitive prophet "sees," is a "seer" of the one God in all things. The unitive prophet feels the ChristLogos in his or her own being and understands that being to be the same being present in the whole created order, universe, Earth, life community, and culture. What if someone spoke for the right to life for plants, animals, and even insects as well as for human young? What if that same person recognized that some people will choose abortion because they feel trapped or raped or coerced into pregnancy and that these people deserve safety in their sad choice? What if the same person stood against capital punishment unless the prisoner him- or herself chose that option over and against life in a cage? What if the same person recognized that samesex couples are what they are and that bothsex couples are what they are? Does having compassion for samesex people in their need for permanent, dignified unions mean that those unions must necessarily be called marriages? If procreativity is part of marriage, then samesex unions are not marriage. But they are unions in love, and unions in love are holy and therefore dignified. What if bothsex people who believe in marriage as one man and one woman are also supported in their beliefs by such a prophet?

What if someone floated a position that supports all that lives and all that supports all that lives? Those caught up in either "left-wing fundamentalisms" or "right-wing fundamentalisms" would feel challenged and equally so. The equally self-righteous poles of this bipolar disorder would be forced to the middle to shake hands and do business. Some will stay stubborn on the left and some on the right. How different, after all, were Stalin and Hitler? Most would, however, move toward the center and express unitive good will and the resultant tolerance. Martin Luther King, Jr. was an angry man, but not a violent man. His anger was a presence and energy in his speeches. That same energy was present in the Hebrew prophet Robert Zimmerman, later called Bob Dylan. In "Blowin' in the Wind," "The Times They Are A-Changin'," "The Lonesome Death of Hattie Caroll," "Oxford Town," "When the Ship Comes In," and many others, the anger of God was sung out with the calling power of spiritual anger. "Enough of this!" was the statement of both of these prophets. "You will stop this—we have had enough" was the call. But, "I have a dream today" was the unitive vision born of the love of God, always present in true prophecy.

What if another "I have a dreamer" spoke out in the name of God? What if that person claimed to be the incarnate anger of God as well as the incarnate bliss and love of God? Wouldn't that person be unsafe to everyone comforted in their bipolar self-righteousness? Would it not be possible for both liberals and conservatives to collude in order to invalidate that person? Would they agree to shoot that person? To crucify that person again? Would they take their places in the conservative Sanhedrin and in the liberal Empire as they did 2000 years ago? The unitive prophet is the true prophet even if it takes his or her crucifixion to unite the opposing poles.

All mystics, Christian or not, know that the whole cosmos, the galaxy, the solar system, and Earth, with all her life systems of air, water, and soil supporting the life community, and the whole of human culture and the trans-spiritual truth embodied in the whole are charged, suffused, and permeated with the very presence of God. How do they know? They know because they feel that presence in the unitive experience within their own beings. The joy of mystics is that unitive experience. The anguish of prophets is the shattered and shattering experience they have with everything surrounding them. To know experientially above anything else that God is One throughout creation and to witness war, casual abortions, ecological devastation, greed, plundering of the poor, mass starvation alongside mass gluttony, and the epidemic of addiction illnesses is the pain that awakens true mysticism and turns it into true prophecy. Prophecy, the proclamation of unitive truth, is the logical extension of unitive or true mysticism. Christ the Mystic becomes Christ the Prophet.

CHAPTER 24

Ecochristology: A Unitive Christology

Put simply, a christology is a way of understanding Christ. There are two christologies traditionally; they are called *descending* and *ascending*. The descending version is the most common and could be summed up in the following way: the Holy Spirit, third person of the Trinity that is God, announces to the girl Mary that she is to be the mother of the Jewish messiah. In the Christian revelation, this messiah is the son of God, second person of the pre-existent Trinity. This would be accomplished by the will of the Father, the first person of that same Trinity. Hence, the Christian understanding of God as triune.

Mary, an unwed Jewish virgin, becomes pregnant with the Christ-child who is born among the animals in a stable in Bethlehem. This Christ-child/messiah, Jesus, grows into a man who between his thirtieth and thirty-third years announces the kingdom of the Father to the Jewish people. At thirty-three, he is betrayed by his student Judas to a collusion of the Jewish and Roman hierarchies. Through a perversion of justice, Jesus is falsely convicted and given capital punishment. Three days later, he rises from the dead and appears again to his women friends/disciples and then to the other male friends/disciples. Not long after that, he ascends to the place from which he descended and once again assumes his transcendent existence with the Father. He promises that the Holy Spirit will descend among his disciples, an event later called Pentecost. The Holy Spirit, then, is promised as the imminent presence of God among Christians.

Ascending christologies differ greatly from the descending model but are still considered to be sound theologically. Chapter 8, on the Jungian rosary, employs this ascending model. In an ascending christology, Jesus of Nazareth, born a man in every way, grows in understanding of his essential self as he matures. In time, he comes to realize his identity with the Father and the Holy Spirit. It is a developmental process, one of progressive realization toward enlightenment. He preaches a new human relationship with the divine, identified as one at the level of being. Being is the name of God in the book of Genesis: "I am who am." Jesus, having evolved into an understanding of his being as ChristLogos, states that he and the Father are one. This ontological (*ontos* is Greek for being) identification with God is deemed heretical by the Jews. The Jewish Sanhedrin (governing body) colludes with the Romans and he is put to death, horribly crucified. He promises the Holy Spirit as comforter and guide. Because God is one though three, the Holy Spirit is the presence of the ChristLogos and is the presence of the Father at the very same time. So, the presence of the Holy Spirit is the presence of the ChristLogos, is the presence of the Father.

I am proposing a third christology, a third way of understanding the presence of Christ. Integrating the opening verses of the Gospel of John with modern evolutionary science, we come up with an ecochristology. In this model, the ChristLogos is identified with and as Godhead transcendent of space and time. I am not suggesting a Godhead prior to Trinity. I am suggesting a one-God model prior to differentiation into triunity. From this transcendence, the ChristLogos is understood to be the presence of creative consciousness, which expresses divine creativity through space/time and energy/matter in an evolving universe. I am holding that the fireball ("In the beginning was the Word"), the emergent galaxies, the solar system, and the planet Earth with her myriad life forms and all human cultures are the many expressions of the one creative consciousness that is the transcendent and imminent God embodied in space and time. ("Through him all things came to be and nothing came to be except through him.") As such, the whole created order, and especially the biospheric ecology of the planet, *IS* the embodied presence of the ChristLogos. Christians are called, therefore, to be the most eco-centric of all humans, of all cultures. Ecochristology is the recognition of the presence of God in all things, making all things sacramental and thus sacred.

To collude in the crucifixion of the life community is to collude in the second crucifixion of Christ. We have done so! But we are a community that believes in and hopes for the resurrection. It is our sacred obligation, then, to be the womb and birth canal of that resurrection. The whole Earth is the stable where both Christ and the animals are sheltered. The whole Earth is Bethlehem. The star of unitive truth is the star we follow toward that realization. Hindus and Buddhists and other "wisemen" from the East are journeying also, and we meet them as brothers and sisters. The true Christian must become the prophet of unity, speaking in defense of the soil, the air, the water, and all living beings of this planet, the stable of third-millennium Christianity. As the very soul of Christianity languishes and is shrinking in the midst of a form no longer able to adequately present the ChristLogos to the world, our belief in death and resurrection becomes even more important and poignant. The new wine will not fit into the old wineskins, and this is why the churches appear so sterile and lame. Third-millennium Christianity will require new wineskins. The third-millennium Christian will be that new wineskin.

CHAPTER 25

The Mystic in the Modern World:
An Invitation to Mature Christianity

The modern Western world is a culture bursting with material glut, while at the same time starving and anorexic with meaninglessness. Imagine one of those jukeboxes from the fifties turned up full blast and playing Jimi Hendrix's "Foxy Lady." The screws are rattling loose and parts are falling off, but still the music continues twenty-four hours a day. Most everything we own is beeping and buzzing. People pass by with cell phones at their ears, seeming to be talking with themselves. People with ear-phoned iPods are equally isolated in their own worlds of hip-hop or whatever. People work on laptop computers around the clock and in any location. The cars are faster, fancier, and higher-tech. And the meaninglessness of all this is so painful that relief is sought in a growing plethora of addictions. The need for noise and distraction itself is an addiction, locking each of us into our own lonely world, our own sub-universe. The unraveling and meaninglessness are exacerbated by the addictive substances used to self-medicate, causing the need for more addictions. The circle of glut, meaninglessness, addiction, further glut, and further meaninglessness continues and deepens by the day.

Coming back from a speaking trip about a year ago, I was in a large, urban airport. There was a large room with several hundred fixed chairs all facing a large screen with CNN playing. People were here and there throughout the room, each with some empty seats on all sides as though protecting him- or herself from contact. They were all talking, and none to each other. They all wore ear attachments for cell phones or were talking directly into their phones. It was like a surrealist painting. CNN was "blah blah blahing" with explosions and carnage. There was laughter, loud talk, serious talk—and not one person was speaking to another in the room. I thought to myself, "North America is a giant insane asylum!"

The glut and the addiction causing further glut are all at the expense of the planet. The planet is unraveling. The life systems of air, water, soil, and species are more and more disrupted as the demand upon them deepens. The life community and the human community embedded in it experience greater stress with each passing day. Bomb here; storm there. The Earth is one system. The family frays, the culture frays, the community of life frays. "The American lifestyle is not up for discussion," says President Bush. Oh?

As we gaze out from the windows of our truly hideous (not to mention wasteful and more-macho-than-thou) Hummers, a growing portion of humanity goes without the basic necessities of life. Like the crowds swelling outside the Russian palace in 1917, there is huge resentment against the West generally, but against the United States in particular. The starving will always resent the glutton. Terrorism is one outward expression of this resentment. Islam is not without its own insanities, to be sure, and we did have to respond to 9/11. However, if we are ever to heal the hatred rather than bomb the symptoms, we must deal with the epidemic resentment spawned by our addicted and addictive lifestyles. Our lifestyles *are* open to discussion after all! All addictions are counterfeit searches for satisfaction. We must find a basis for satisfaction that is not addictive. Life does offer legitimate satisfactions and abundant prosperity. Unbounded growth is cancer. Terrorism has become like a collective form of AIDS. Ultimately, it will break down the culture's will to resist it. We broadcast our hideous statistics: 66 percent of us are overweight, with half of that being morbidly obese. The terrorists are not unaware of this softness.

As a bicultural institution, the family is in tatters. We comfort ourselves with lies. The idea that divorce is "better for the children" is an evil lie. Unless there is overt addiction with its many attendant forms of violence, it is better for children if their mother and father grow up, take responsibility for their problems, and respond to the lives they have engendered. The family is the psychic nest of human young. Children are without rights to prevent the destruction of their one and only family, one and only nest. It is a biological and cultural crime to strip a child of his or her own family for anything but the most extreme reasons. Children have the right to life, liberty, and family. With the coming of age of the baby boomers, we have had forty years of adolescence in this country; many of the young have never known a real adult. Their deaths by suicide and addiction are the ghastly affirmation of this total confusion. Many born after 1970 have no frame of reference to even understand the dimensions of their problem. When the sea of pain and despair becomes too large, when no shores can be seen in any direction, they take the only way out. And these are those we have "chosen" to survive the womb! Shame on us all! And always "with the help of Almighty God" and "May God bless America" dribbling from our lips. Again, shame on us all!

To the prominent voices of the left and right fundamentalisms—and we all know who they are: It is time to be quiet. We are tired of these blowhards looking for the next opportunity to appear relevant—they are of no help to us anymore. Thank you for your service and please be quiet! There is a God of the inside and a God of the outside, and they are of course the same God. The God of the inside of a culture is represented by the traditions of that nation or culture. This is a rather tame God, spoonfed to us by many sincere and dedicated people. In all four vehicles of Christianity—Catholicism, Orthodoxy, Reformation Protestantism, and evangelical/fundamentalism—this version of God has gone lukewarm, even dead cold. What W. B. Yeats said in his

poem *The Second Coming* has come to be: "The best lack all conviction and the worst are filled with passionate intensity." The former
can be thought of as left-wing fundamentalists and the latter as right-
wing fundamentalists. The model itself is burned out, lacks calling
power, and needs to have a funeral—and then a resurrection.

But there is also a God of the outside of cultures. That God can
only be met by those who are willing or are forced outside of the
culture, those who close the door and go on a journey. Outsiders
are those called to meet the wild God who has no name, and has
many names. Those who make that journey "lose their lives in order
to gain them." The wild God, once met, gives the outsider a name
with which to return to the culture. Members of the culture, more
often than not, are all involved with the niceties and details of the
insider God. Usually, though not always, they despise and even kill
the outsider who returns to them with a message from the God of
the outside. Jesus was one such outsider. He returned with the name
Abba (Papa) and was not welcome. We may now return with the
ubiquitous ChristLogos. There are others. In the following poem by
Paul Weiss of Bar Harbor, Maine, we hear the voice of the God of the
outside: "Those with ears to hear, let them hear."

You Hold This

I.

The four-year-old asks his father if he can help him
fix the car. And the father hands him a wrench
and says, "Yes, you hold this. Give it to me when I ask."
We have each been given something to hold,
and it connects us to the whole. That is all

I watch how easily my attention shifts from the 'moment'
I have been given to hold to the wide-screen cinerama of the world,
its surround-sound urgency and pain. And I wander into

the guilty nightmare of the child who watches the car careen
out of control and wonders, "Did I hold the wrench right?"

2.

At six-thirty the sun is breaking over the white horizon,
lifting above the low hills over my frozen yard—
the cracking maples, the shriveled rhododendron leaves
playing possum with winter, the garbage cans full
and iced over. Westward I watch the first anointing of
the trees as sun drinks up the last of the gray-blue land.
From the east it skids and bounces through the woods
off the glazed snow. The red squirrel leaves no tracks
as he shuttles across the warp of sunlight and shadow. The
spruce and hemlocks move barely from a place so perfectly
not other than the cold, as if inhabiting a space
that's smaller and emptier than the air. I fill my
swaying thistle feeder to the brim. A goldfinch signals,
and his mates descend. The way things are is what there is.
The way things are that holds us, and is held.

3.

Sunlight and shadow is the mind's own dance.
I am reptile, mammal, and something provisionally human
and still to come. The lizard's eye sees only the shadow world
of life and death, advance and retreat. The mammal learns
to care about its losses, ache for its young. As human,
I advance, retreat, ache for my young—and for my youth—
for infinite time to master the infinite creative task. (The boy
is growing old.) The heart turns with the great earth,
the brain widens to include the space that births it,
awareness unfolding beyond all light and shadow; and hands,
becoming empty of themselves, touch like the velvet
of the rain against the velvet earth.

4.

We are this truth that rises from the earth and is made
of stars, laid folded in the brain and to be wooed back
into divine embrace. Outrage strips the skin of its sweet
touching. Fear shrinks the brain's horizon from revealed
transparency—a blue sky happily surprised by rain,
the green lady laughing into bloom—into a lonely bunker
lined with hapless panels of control that override the
heart's design to touch and celebrate. Shock is enshrined.
And grief that sinks and does not pollinate the spring
betrays itself into the hands of hate. Why are our children
lying in the marketplace in pieces? Why do the fathers
not return home? Why are the women pulled from their
houses screaming? This is not Iraq. This is a slow
motion cry that happens over centuries, a stifled wail
disfiguring our native face as ancient waves of grief,
disguised as policy, disguised as faith, wash over continents
and collide. We cannot fathom the shape of our own
claws tearing our own flesh, tearing at the earth, snaking
through our common dream, ever replacing the
tamboura and the flute with the sirens of empire,
complacencies of greed and conquest, the oiled whirr of
the boardroom sucking with long straws the blood and birth
waters of the world. How to speak, how to ripen or restrain,
how to doctor, how to hold the wrench? The heart learns
to break and reaffirm as an eternal recurrence, to be
ground as sesame paste into the dirt, to seed and rise again
under the tanks and laptops of the warriors.

5.

The frozen snow gives way to mud and mists of April—
slowly, slowly in Maine, we hang between two worlds.
Winter's suppressed howl can't hasten the new leaves.

The indeterminate cold makes no bargains. It is the season
of suicide. We burn our final fat into the unknown hour
of awakening warmth. We burn our dreams to hurry
the morning light. But the rising year is not the year we
have known. The mud is not the old mud of our April
expectations. Even the darkness speaks with a different
voice, is not the darkness we were sure of. We are wandering
in a world that changed even while we were walking.
The floorboards were replaced under our very steps, and we
the old ones are dazed and uncertain. We flounder between
two worlds, wondering why our old configurations falter,
offended by the failure of our ideals, making the failure
personal, aghast at our collaboration, not knowing how
to withdraw our own feet from the gas pedal of our
final descent, even as spring shoots faithfully press forth
into the shaky air. We have slipped through the doorway
of irreversible calamity. It is not the success of our dreams
but the resiliency of our roots that we are now forced
to flesh, like cliffside pines, alchemists of rock and wind,
squandering no soil. Knowing ourselves. The coal
of our old calculations must be pressed to new diamond.
I become a sacrifice to living presence, to inclusive seeing,
to the largeness of my own heart, to the wisdom of my
smallest root, to the truth of my next word. I become
an ancient camel path. I listen for the approaching bells.

6.

I lean against my staff like a boy holding the wrench.
No one has asked me to fix this car.
The earth spreads out slowly from where I stand.
A field of relations spreads out from this heart.
My ear has been tutored to hear, my voice to speak.
I look at what I have been asked to hold.

I pour this tea with you in mind. All is awake
and present in the offering. Embracing time
and timelessness I am at a crossroads of
multidimensional space, of absolute relation,
from which I will not retreat. I will hold.
Not an eyebrow will flinch from this delicate balance
of press and take I share with all things; from this
emptiness ready to say "I," from this love ready
to say "you." From the messy and sublime intimacy
of holding the shared space, of birthing the divine
play, the paradox of form and suffering. Like
children in the storm of Golgotha we look up to
the person on the cross and ask "Can I help?" And
passing us his sacred heart, he says "Yes. You hold this."

PAUL WEISS

The religious establishment—exhausted by the four-way argument,
insecure about its own methods, confused about the very issues at
hand, taking limp cues from political correctness, the "mental health"
establishment, and academia, or else shrinking into outright insistence
with rolled-up sleeves—lacks the real faith, the real conviction, and,
therefore, the psychic energy to inform the culture it has formed. If
it cannot inform, it cannot transform. Entrenched and arthritic religious hierarchies—defensive and too often peopled by well-meaning
misfits and sometimes by thinly disguised perverts—find themselves
mired down in controversy, human weakness, power-brokering, trivial
theological squabbles, and other tangential issues. In many instances,
the only identities people gain from any one of the four vehicles is
that it makes them feel different and "correct" when up against argu-
ments from any of the other three vehicles. The result is a deepening
of left-wing and right-wing fundamentalisms. Our best energies are
"off-gassed" in squabbles of no significance that only worsen our

deepest concerns rather than resolving them. There were *three* crosses on Calvary, not one or two. There was a little man on one cross, a slightly larger one on the other, and the universal presence of God reaching out to both of them from the center. Little men, polarize, while the great man reconciles from the center and unites.

We need a post-denominational, third-millennium Christianity. Instead of five centuries of arguing about justification by faith versus justification by works, only to admit that they both play a part in the equation, *OBVIOUSLY,* we need a living ChristLogos who appeals to the young and answers their real questions about addiction, sexuality, the family, the environment, meaning, the future, and so on. Most important, we need to speak sincerely, speak the truth from the heart, and then do the truth. And my fellow boomers, we must end "boomer-speak," the use of language to mask the truth—to spin. Yes, "I'm talkin' about my generation."

Again, we must put an absolute end to boomer-speak and use language to reveal truth rather than obscure it. A nation of aging liars and of young people who have had little experience of truth leads to disaster, to the "abomination of desolation." We should hope and pray as we age that those who come after us will be more generous than we have been to them, those among them we have allowed to survive the womb. The God of the outside is once again knocking at the door. "Do we have the ears to hear?" We stare into the hell of global ecological catastrophe. Only truth, felt truth rather than stiff ideologies, will allow our souls to awaken. Our souls—buried beneath lies, denial, half-truths, spin, addiction, greed, and rage—await our response. Only an emptied and addiction-free Christianity will allow the individual and collective Christian soul to rise from the dead and restore us to sanity and health. A restored soul will desire the life of other-service rather than self-service. We will hear the cries of the poor, our own poor, and the poor of other nations. A restored soul will feel the pain we pour over the animals, plants, and their global habitat. This is third-millennium Christianity. When the ChristLogos awakens among us, Christian mystics will become Christian prophets.

So, then, the "invitation to mature Christianity." Wherever we find ourselves is where we are! Regardless of what vehicle of Christianity we find ourselves in, we should remain, if possible. To receive the God of outsiders through modern Christian mysticism and be the door that allows the new breath inside, we begin the transformation of Christianity in the third millennium. A transformed, third-millennium Christianity will bring that new breath, that new spirit, into the culture. The new breath will revive the dead culture with new vision, new purpose, new life. I invite you to return to the chapters on prayer (Part II) and to review the deep meanings in those prayers. If you are moved to do so, kneel down right now, alone or among others, and surrender your life to the ChristLogos, and join the rest of us who are attempting to build a new culture. If you choose to, you can add your name to the list on www.albertjlachance.com. In time, if enough join the worldwide Church of Christ the Mystic, we will post a map online to show the location where each of you lives so that you may find each other and gather for liturgies of silence. In doing so, we will be creating a unitive approach to the presence of God.

CHAPTER 26

The Fourth Voice:
ChristLogos and the Voices of the Brain

Recently, in the field of psychology, there has been considerable attention paid to what is called the triune brain. The idea is that the human brain has three major or general structural levels, or components.

The outer brain, often called interchangeably the neocortex or neomammalian cortex, is the seat of the major cognitive processes, especially thought. Elsewhere, I have called it the *cognitive cortex* and will do so here. Each of the structural levels can be said to have a voice and the voice of the cognitive cortex is thought. Beneath the cognitive cortex and enclosed within it is what is called the paleo-mammalian cortex, or limbic system. This second brain is the seat of the affective or emotional functions of the brain. We could say that the voice of the *affective cortex,* as I call it, is affect or emotion. We share this level of brain with the other mammals, one and all. It provides us with the ability to communicate ("whisper") with horses, dogs, cats, other primates, and so on. In Christian iconography, the function of this brain has its venue in the "sacred heart," the fourth chakra for Hindus. For the Chinese, the heart of the human is considered the heart of the cosmos, the place where the universe feels itself. And deep in the core of the human brain is buried the third brain, the brain stem, also called the *reptilian cortex*. It is called "reptilian" in that it represents the same level of psychic functioning as a snake or reptile. That level of functioning is primitive, instinctual. In Hinduism, the spinal cord is called the *kundalini*—literally, serpent. So, the human, from the point of view of brain biology, is a triune creature. We include and manifest all levels of chordate animal life, from the earliest reptilian to the mammalian and the primate. The three voices of the one brain become one voice, the voice of the human.

There is, however, a fourth voice, a fourth dimension to human awareness. That voice could be called the voice of awareness itself. If the reptilian brain stem is transcended by and included in the limbic system, and the limbic system is transcended by and included in the cognitive cortex, then the three voices are transcended and included in awareness itself. Awareness is the medium within which we experience our felt instinctual signals, our affective responses, and our thoughts. Awareness is the presence of the soul. If the soul is understood to be the local venue or subset of the nonlocal ChristLogos, then the fourth voice within us is the voice of God present throughout the created order. The fourth voice is often unheard amidst the noise of thinking, feeling, and intuiting—but it is there!

What is often called "enlightenment" is the progressive quieting of the three brain voices in order that the softer but more universal fourth voice can be heard. When only the fourth voice is heard, the egoic self formed of the chattering of the three brains shatters and the self of the ChristLogos becomes the real self of the enlightened person. Awareness progressively awakens in the realization of being the nontemporal, nonspatial medium, or self in which thoughts, feelings, and instincts are experienced. We live in the strangest paradox. In our own heartbeat and breathing, in our experience of days and nights and the seasons of the planet, we hear the tick-tock, tick-tock of time. In awareness, however, we experience ourselves as transcendent of time and even of space. Meditation and Eucharist can lead us to the realization that the cosmos itself is our real self. When awareness becomes aware of itself in us, we arrive at the awakening of our oneness with the whole, and we even transcend the whole and experience our oneness with the source or the origin of the universe itself! We come to see that awareness is birthless and deathless. We come to see that the awareness that is the voice of our deepest souls is the presence of the ChristLogos. We can then see that the three voices of the brain die with the brain. They are truly dust and truly do return to dust. Awareness, however, is the presence of the ChristLogos and does not die when the body dies. Nor was it born when the body was conceived and later born. But most of us, "distracted from distraction by distraction," seldom listen to the fourth voice. We are seldom able to listen to the fourth voice in the world we have created around ourselves. We seldom listen, then, to who we really are!

When we have evolved sufficiently to be able to differentiate between the voices that scream "I am the body, I am my thoughts, I am my feelings and instincts," and the one that whispers "I am," we transcend the death of the body and of the brain. We are then ready to experience our identity, as was Jesus when he said, "I and the Father are one," and when Paul said, "I no longer live, but Christ lives in me." When we experience our oneness with the ChristLogos, the manifest dimension of the Father, we too then awaken to our oneness with the Father whose name is "I am who Am," whose name is Being. We come to see that the fourth voice is the one voice, the voice of the Father. We come to hear that voice in the night sky, in the Earth, and in all her life forms. We come to hear the same voice in the many languages of the sacred, the voices of the religions of all cultures. In awakening to the one voice, we find ourselves at home with God whether we are alive or dead. We are in the communion of all the saints.

CHAPTER 27

The American Experience:
The Unitive Experiment of God

In the 2006 elections in the United States, the American people soundly rejected an ideological system presented by the so-called "neo-conservative" Republicans over the last several years. That ideological system included a co-opting of Christian language in order to serve a narrow and greedy minority posing as the "true Christians" of this country. The "Christianity" they presented to us was in fact a blasphemy of the intentions of Jesus Christ in the Gospels. After having ravaged the presidency of Bill Clinton in a twisted and judgmental assault on his sexual weaknesses, they tried to present themselves as a sort of American *perestroika,* or spiritual awakening. (Not once did we hear the president's assailants commend Hillary Clinton for her willingness to suffer in order to preserve the vow of her marriage—a truly "Christian" act on her part.) Ignoring Jesus' stern warnings about judgment, they used the impeachment mechanisms of the U.S. Constitution to serve an aggressive and truly fascistic money and power lust. This, notwithstanding Jesus' even more strident warnings regarding the accumulation of wealth and refusal to serve the poor and the vulnerable.

Calling themselves neo-conservatives and hiding behind that euphemism, this small group of nominal Republicans were in fact not Republican at all, but more closely resembled a new kind of fascism. The fury driving the judgmentalism and greed could be compared to aggressive cancer cells as they multiply and divide without controls.

Many Christians drawn from all four vehicles of Christianity bought into the neo-conservative rhetoric and subsequently abandoned the balance and eloquence inherent in true Republican politics. Considering that Abraham Lincoln, Dwight Eisenhower, Gerry Ford, both Elizabeth and Bob Dole, and John McCain are Republicans, these people bore very little resemblance to true Republicanism. The country went into a numbing spell, the spell of the Big Lie. Both Stalin and Hitler knew that if you make the Big Lie big enough, ubiquitous enough, people are stunned into silence.

As "conservatives," they conserved nothing. Even willing to consider the consummate stupidity of disrupting the fragile Arctic wilderness for six months' or a year's worth of fuel, these people reversed community gains in ecology made over several decades and several administrations. American corporations were encouraged to produce atrocities such as the Hummer while the Japanese quietly developed hybrid technologies. In the spell of the Big Lie we marched dreamlike into war with Iraq. Oil junkies that we are, we became more and more willing to mug any country that won't give us a fix. Beginning with the amiable President Reagan, the neo-cons quickly devolved into truly foul people such as Newt Gingrich and Karl Rove. The true spirit of America is presently awakening—and just in time.

There is, nonetheless, a distinct role for true, unitive Christian spirituality when one thinks of the American nation as a unitive experiment of God. We read on the U.S. dollar *e pluribus unum,* Latin for "out of the many, one." The United States is a gathering of every race, every creed, every nation on this planet into a single system of law and personal dignity. As we realize the ecological, economic, and technological oneness of the planet, we can begin to measure the dimensions of our cultural failure at oneness. The United States is the divine prototype of a planet at peace in its diversity and oneness. By bringing together all peoples of Earth, we are offered the opportunity to forge a oneness among the many. Our external differences bridged by our internal subjectivities lead to a transcendent union or communion among us. The subjectivities identified across cultural differences will allow for a trans-cultural experience of The One.

The mission of true American Christians is to identify the internal subjectivities common to Judaism, Christianity, and Islam. These can be called the Abrahamic subjectivities. These, then, can be identified with their counterparts in the Hindu-Buddhist and Taoist-Confucian as well as the tribal-shamanic traditions. In this discovery and experience of those internal subjectivities we can distill from the American experience those principles that can form a model for peace (not without conflict) among the various religions first and then among the various nations of the world. From the United States of America to a United Nations of Earth—this is the divine calling of this great nation.

Those who in the name of God, in the name of Christ, in the name of Allah, emphasize differences and divisions among the cultures sin against the spirit that is the founding inspiration of this nation. The formula goes: Out of the one, the many, out of the many, the one. As with all ideologies of fear, greed, and cultural superiority, neo-cons and all such self-seekers derail the true mission of God and of the American people in order to stuff their own coffers with our collective wealth and our destiny. It is wise for us to remember Mussolini's statement, later quoted by Robert F. Kennedy, Jr., that fascism was a misnomer for what Germany and Italy were trying to become. The real name, he asserted, was "corporatism." When Christian rhetoric is made to serve individual or corporate greed, Jesus is made to serve Caesar.

A friend and colleague of mine, Episcopal priest Adrian Robbins-Cole, once described fundamentalism as the use of religious language and symbols to separate one religious or cultural system from another. Using the truth to lie, in other words, the end result is the separation of persons from persons. Fear is the tool used to maintain the separation. He went on to say that the antidote for fundamentalism is the willingness to research those other religions and cultures in order to identify in them the truths also found in one's own. Truth unifies and falsehood separates. The American people seem to be deciding to stop tolerating the misuse and heretical misuse of Christianity. They seem to be abandoning corporatism and greed in deference to becoming whole again. They seem to be realigning their wills to the will of God's Great Experiment. The world waits eagerly again for dialogue rather than distortion. The American people are moving toward the politics of decency.

The Politics of Decency

When we gather up the insights contained in the prophetic tradition, drawn from both the Hebrew Bible and the New Testament, it all amounts to what I like to call the politics of decency. Decency is being among one's family, friends, and neighbors. Decency is the embrace of differences, sensitivities, and the oneness of those we call our own. Decency would then extend beyond the immediate circle of our lives to other political and religious systems. Always, decency seeks to identify what unites us rather than what divides us while nonetheless admitting the divisions and differences.

Decency must next be extended beyond our own ecclesiastical communities and embrace the interiorities of others in their approach to the Absolute. Still further, the politics of decency must extend toward other life forms in the recognized rights of animals, plants, insects—rights to habitat, to sunlight, air, water, and soil. The politics of decency would be extended toward the planet Earth herself. The politics of decency would next recognize the pre-born, admitting that, regardless of what the Supreme Court has said, abortion is always a tragedy and should be avoided whenever possible through moral education. All conceptions would be acknowledged to be divine events, the eruption of eternity into time, and all pregnant and child-rearing mothers, regardless of economic circumstances or marital status, would be supported in their work for at least the first five years of their children's lives. Decency would extend to those who, after being aware of their alternatives, still choose to go forward with abortions. *Roe v. Wade* and similar legislation would at least offer clean and medically safe abortions for these women. As we do with consciousness-raising movements about alcohol, tobacco, drugs, and other detrimental and counterproductive issues and behaviors, we would be relentless in raising consciousness regarding the tragic choice of abortion. The politics of decency would extend to everyone, regardless of their starting point. We are indeed born equal but unfortunately the equality ends there. There are those who will die from smoking, from drinking, and from drugs. There are those who will never arise to human consciousness that includes their own offspring; they are not at fault.

Still, it would be myopic and immature to omit from the politics of decency the politics of responsibility. The perpetrators of crime in the White House, in Congress, in the courts, as well as in the corporations or in the streets, must be held accountable to their victims. Presidents who attack other nations in thinly designed attempts to maraud for oil should face the consequences of their actions. Congressional representatives and senators likewise who broker their power for personal gain need to be held accountable. Corrupt judges and lawyers, from the Supreme Court down, should face impeachment by those who uncover their corruption. How do we trust our supreme tribunals of justice if those ascending to those benches lie in order to get there? Is our final defense against the power of the state to be in the hands of liars who work for the state? Corporate heads earning several hundred times their workers' wages have stolen from those same workers.

But decency must extend even to those convicted of criminal behavior. Should we seek revenge through capital punishment? Perhaps those convicted of capital crimes should themselves be given a choice. Perhaps they could choose life without parole or some form of capital punishment such as injection. In that way, they, and not the society they violated, would be choosing the method of recompense. In any case, decency would be fair treatment toward all that lives, human or nonhuman.

CHAPTER 28

The Ten Fingers of Hell: Addiction, Recovery, and Redemption

Christianity has traditionally given considerable focus to the sinfulness of human nature and to God's efforts at redemption or reunion. Presently, much of the Western world finds itself caught up in a widespread cultural pathology. That pathology could be called an epidemic of addiction illness. It is the modern equivalent of the plague. Addiction illness, perhaps more often than not, drives the behavior of what we have called sin. Mysticism is made impossible by active addiction, in that any addiction cuts off the experience of the essential or unitive self. Addiction is an illness and therefore not a moral issue. However, the behaviors driven by addiction illness are moral issues and, frequently, legal issues as well. It is pointless to rant and rave about sin without addressing the underlying cause of the behavior called sin.

To feel separated from one's true self, from others, from the life community, Earth, the universe, and God, is a fearsome experience. We rupture into a place called addiction-space, which does not really exist and yet is real. Much like cyberspace, it has no geographical location, yet it exists as an extension of the collective human psyche. To exist in addiction-space requires a dependence upon the addiction that first brought us there. Because it is a world of fear, all addictions are then a response to fear that the addiction itself has caused. Like Satan frozen at the center of Dante's hell, at the core of all addiction illness is this paralyzing fear. Fear is the shadow of faith, the absence of the light and love of God. When people live in chronic fear, they will eventually become open to any relief whatsoever. Addiction is the attempt to assuage the pain of fear by introducing a false god into the soul to relieve it. Alcohol, street drugs, prescription drugs, nicotine, somatic chemistries of lust, gambling, and food addiction, cyber and media addictions, consumerism generally, oil and greed addiction specifically—the list continues to grow. The horrible fact to remember is that the need to assuage the fear was caused by the addiction itself. Recovery from addiction requires withdrawal from the false god by calling on the presence of the real God of the ChristLogos. This is done through surrender. Through surrender we move from addiction-space to reality, to where God lives.

Christianity seems to struggle in grasping that God really does love us in our sinfulness. When we understand that "missing the mark" was the Hebrew understanding of sin, we can see why. No parent condemns or damns a child for missing the mark. We struggle with our sinfulness, which is exactly what he did not want us to do! Whores, tax collectors, criminals—these were his friends of choice right up to the crucifixion! Don't resist evil; instead do good, was his divine advice. Good displaces evil as light displaces shadow. Am I saying that he wants us to live in ever-deepening wrongdoing? Of course not. He wanted and wants us to surrender, and then allow his love to dispel the sin. When we light a candle, we do not have to push the darkness out of the room. The candle's light itself dispels the darkness. His presence is the candle within, the essential self.

We could say that sin is the measure of our inability to behave in satisfactory ways at all times. Now it is obvious that as addiction progresses, inability also progresses, and the behaviors as a result become worse. Buddhists use the term *dukkha,* which translates as "unsatisfactory" and sometimes as "suffering." Everything and everyone suffers from not being fully satisfactory. The first of the Four Noble Truths reads that all life includes dukkha, which is not only a function of our humanity, but a function of life itself. The second of the Four Noble

Truths says that the cause of suffering is craving, which is the most obvious symptom of addiction. The third Truth is that suffering ends when craving ends. Recovery begins to happen when craving ends, but how? The Fourth Noble Truth is that craving ends when we follow the Eight-Fold Path. Right view, right resolve or commitment, right speech, right action, right livelihood, right effort or discipline, right mindfulness, right concentration—these are the ways of the Eight-Fold Path. They could serve as a description of the recovered or redeemed life. The recovered life is life redeemed from the hell that is addiction-space.

If sin is a function of our humanity, displacement of sin by truth is a function of our inherent divinity. Willingness is accomplished by surrender. When we give up the struggle to be good, self-righteously, the ChristLogos transfigures us into goodness. We cannot will our goodness; we already *are* goodness! A willed spirituality is a contradiction in terms. Spirituality is measured by a progressive surrender of the will. Willed righteousness is self-righteousness, as noted above. It is a product of the ego-mask, an attempt to look good. Right effort is surrender leading to humility and wholeness and, thus, goodness, being good.

Addiction, not sin, is crippling modern Christianity. Addiction in its many, its "legion" forms, has enfeebled the Church in its attempt to provide guidance for the very culture it has spawned. The sickness of the culture is responsible for the sickness of the ecosystems in which it is embedded. Addiction must be named so that recovery and redemption can begin. I belonged to churches in which there were several three- or even four-hundred-pound people. One of them literally ate herself to death, rupturing internally under her own weight and bleeding to death internally. Others in the community came to church with flushed faces, purple noses, and reeking of alcohol. They, and others like them, are all dying one day at a time, and little or nothing is said. There are cocaine addicts, prescription addicts, gambling addicts, and sex addicts among the ordained and the non-ordained.

Then there are the religious addictions themselves, rigid and judg-mental "praising the Lord" and enslaved to the somatic chemistries of compulsive devotion. Fundamentalisms of all kinds are not religion, they are mental illness. When we say "Praise the Lord," often we get the same feeling as when a pot-smoker says, "Oh wow man!" There are hierarchy addicts driven by fear, addicted to control, lonely and desperate. There are cyber addicts and consumer addicts and again, little or nothing is said from the pulpit about addiction.

Addiction is the great crippler of the human soul, individually and collectively. If there is a devil, his presence is most clearly seen in the trick of keeping Christianity focused on puny little sins while addiction kills our young, our culture, and our planet. I have known fundamentalists who pride themselves in campaigns against Hallow-een trick or treating, Christmas trees, or the Easter Bunny because of their "pagan" origins. Plato and Aristotle were pagans and they each fueled 1,000 years of Christianity! Whole life systems fray and collapse, species are forced into extinction by the thousands, half of humanity is hungry, pollution poisons life itself—and we are con-cerned with the Eastern Bunny! We stalk clowns while Nazis roam the streets. Fundamentalism—Muslim, Christian, or otherwise—is religious addiction, diagnosable mental illness. Christians would do well to allow Christ to deal with our sin while with Christ we face the demonic lure of addiction.

CHAPTER 29

Samesex Unions and Abortion:
Two Separative Issues and a Unitive Response

Transcend and include! Transcend and include! Developmental psychology, spirituality, and moral development can be summed up in those two words: *transcend* and *include*. We grow by transcending one level of understanding or consciousness in order to then include it at the next level we reach. New information, new insight, gets added and in time, again, we transcend and include the former in a still greater whole. There may come a time when the issues of samesex union and abortion will not be contentious issues operating at the forefront of the Christian community and manipulated by political charlatans to their own cunning ends. However, at the time of the writing of this book, they are at the forefront of the pain that plagues us all. I have complained both privately and professionally about authors who evade dealing with these issues because they wish to avoid the controversy that might threaten book sales. The Buddhist Thich Nhat Hanh in his book *Transformations at the Base* is a refreshing exception to this avoidance.

Third-millennium Christians, especially mystics, must help to transcend the crippling bipolar divisiveness of these two issues. We must transcend the divisions in order to arrive at compassion, for only compassion can be called a Christian position. Can we transcend our bipolar battle lines, transcend both ideological camps in order to grow? To include one another? I think we must! But, before we find a "third option" we must cool the ideological flames and breathe deeply. Option three will be the product of new information, new insight, new understanding—a new level of consciousness.

Below, I look at both issues from a unitive perspective. I am going to try to create a demilitarized zone, or DMZ, and I ask forbearance from each reader. I hope that slowly, together, we might walk through the flames to a cooler and more unitive ground. I ask you to believe in my good intentions, and I ask the same of every reader. I will remind us all from time to time to stop and breathe. I call upon the presence of the ChristLogos present in us as we proceed. I ask that each of you do the same.

Samesex Unions

In Chapter 17 on the rite of sexual love, marriage, I outlined a position that rested on the joining of DNA as the biological half of a bio-cultural, bio-spiritual ritual of joining. I attempted to break the black-and-white framing of the issue of pre-marital sex. I noted that the giving and receiving of physical pleasure is not the same as the act of intercourse with its implications of DNA exchange, new human life, and the future of the species. I am holding that the exchange of DNA is the nucleus around which mating-specific behaviors are constellated. I believe this is the same in all species. Whether an ant, a beetle, a bird, a reptile, a marine or land mammal, all species exhibit ritual forms of behavior preceding and leading to the exchange of DNA.

We could call mating-specific behavior the "language" of procreation. We humans, being self-reflexive, are capable of separating the biological from the cultural dimensions of the ritual. But, if all cultures have such rituals embedded in their traditions, and I believe they do, then this itself indicates some basic repeatability, some basic truth at the species level, at the biological level. Whether or not we believe in evolution, it is clear that there must be a reason for the universal presence of such rituals. Perhaps it is simply that the young of our species need permanent union for optimal functioning. Permanent unions formed for human pleasure, human fulfillment, and procreation are called marriages. We can conceive of permanent unions that do not include procreation. Please continue breathing deeply!

From the conservative side: The most conservative Christian position regarding extra-marital sex holds that it is sinful, even evil. Much neurotic guilt and shame have been heaped on people due to this position over the years, but nonetheless it remains the core teaching in many denominations. Presently, for good or ill, these denominations seem to be a distinct minority in the overall culture that we call the West. Sadly, and perhaps in some part due to the shrinkage in numbers of those who hold this position, the sacramental dimension of the mating ritual has in some ways been separated from the biological or bio-sexual behavior of bothsex couples. The result might be a de-sacralizing of, a vulgarization of, the exchange of DNA, the Word of God in flesh, the BioLogos. Driven by fear for their children, fear for the future of the culture, concern for the pre-born and for other reasons, the fury-driven judgmentalism from the conservatives often further exacerbates the de-sacralization already happening among liberals. Judgment often causes a response of stubbornness because for every action there really is an equal and opposite reaction. As we sow, so we reap.

Conservative Christians also disregard the simple truth that Christ said not one word about homosexual behaviors in the Gospels. Thus, they are forced to appeal to the Old Testament in search of a scriptural basis for their judgments. About judgment, however, Jesus was very clear! Given the warnings about judgment, we should hold suspect any judgment that does not come directly from Jesus' teachings. Still, conservatives rightly have a fundamental intuition that the spiritual depth inherent in the transmission of life is being trivialized and flattened in the loss of the religious dimension of our mating ritual. Further, those with a bothsex orientation often feel a certain dissonance toward behaviors associated with a samesex orientation. Those with a samesex orientation might experience similar dissonance toward bothsex behaviors. These feelings of disgust can often toxify judgments drawn from the Old Testament and elsewhere and can push judgment into open condemnation and even outright hatred and violence. That condemnation, deeply painful, can excite a response in kind from those who are both samesex and Christian.

From the liberal side: Many liberal forms of Christianity seem to have essentially capitulated on their teaching responsibility regarding human sexuality. Only thirty years ago, unmarried couples, cohabitating couples, not-yet-divorced or remarried couples, and samesex couples certainly would have found themselves very uncomfortable in most mainline Christian denominations. Presently, there seems to be a "don't ask, don't tell" policy in many of these churches. In some, there is little to distinguish between the secular culture and the "religious culture" regarding this issue. Practicing Christians in many denominations seem to actually expect their children to be sexually active at a young age and to be living with boyfriends and girlfriends in their twenties or even earlier. While the biological dimension of sexual love can be controlled through various contraceptives, the loss of the cultural dimension brings with it some devastating realities that many attempt to ignore or deny. Among these is the loss of proper ritual bonding, which continues to contribute to the disintegration of the family. The family in breakdown leads to the disintegration of the culture, with the attendant feelings of despair and an unnamed collective grief. It is no coincidence that as we lose the cultural dimension of mating, the divorce rate does not decline significantly from 50–60 percent.

As divorce is viewed more and more as value-neutral, many have come to see samesex promiscuity as value-neutral as well. If we ourselves abandon our marriages and our children, two, three, and sometimes four times, we tend more and more to withhold our critique of others who do the same. We might also withdraw our expectations of samesex people at the same time. If marriage means little or nothing to bothsex couples, why expect more of our children? Why not agree that samesex unions are marriages as well? Regarding judgment, liberals can be pretty preachy and self-righteous themselves. But sadly, when everything is as good as everything else, standards of behavior continue to diminish. We ask less and less of ourselves and of each other. Somehow, perhaps inexplicably, the sense of the sacred is thereby dimmed. Neither self-righteous judgment nor self-righteous *non*-judgment is working! Then what?

From the unitive position: Most of us are growing weary of the polarizing judgments from both sides. A third option, perhaps not totally pleasant in and of itself, holds the only hope of a way through. If we are all to gain, we must all sacrifice some part of our positions; we must transcend them and include part of the other. Again, my request for forbearance and breathing! The word *compromise* means "to promise with." If Christians are ever to be one though many, if we are to be recognized as his followers by the love we bear for one another, we must com-promise, find a third option beyond the impasse. While human sexuality generally and marriage specifically are not limited to their role in procreation, it cannot be denied that procreation itself is certainly part of what human sexuality is about. Some form of samesex behavior shows up in most, if not in all, species. While this is true, it is also true that propagation in those species is not part of samesex behavior. When the time comes in the sexual cycles of any species for propagation, the mating-specific behaviors that lead to propagation are between males and females. The exchange of DNA for procreation is exclusively between males and females. Samesex unions do not lead to the birth of new individuals in any species that I know of. While the giving and receiving of sexual touch has an intrinsic role to play in bothsex behaviors, it is similar to samesex behaviors in that it does not always have to lead to propagation. If, however, we view marriage as the bio-culturally selected environment for the rearing of human young, then DNA—its union, exchange, and development—has everything to do with marriage, with the mating ritual.

What, then, do samesex and bothsex couples have in common? The need to love and to be loved is the most obvious. The desire for permanence and stability is another. The need for, the desire for, and the pleasure in sexual touch is another, without that touch leading to procreation. But procreativity itself is an undeniable function of the domain of bothsex love. This is true even if the male DNA and the female DNA are stored in a sperm or egg bank. Some man or woman put them there! The joining of DNA for propagation remains in the domain of man plus woman, or bothsex unions.

In countries like the United States where there is a clear separation between religion and government, it seems fair and wholesome that all unions, whether samesex or bothsex, be viewed legally by the state as civil unions. Samesex couples would thus be supported in their attempt to live permanent, stable, and dignified lives. They would be granted the legal right to will their wealth to partners, the right to pass on death benefits, and so on. Most important, they would be legitimized in their unique form of loving. Churches and temples would then be responsible in the context of their own theologies and traditions to determine who can and who cannot call themselves married in the theological sense. There are black churches, Latino churches—why not samesex churches? Each person, each couple, and each denomination would be forced to wrestle with the religious meaning of marriage and that volatile issue could be removed from the political debate altogether. Samesex theology would have a good starting point with a three-male Trinity!

When looking at samesex sexuality through the lens of bothsex sexuality, samesex behaviors can appear to some as disordered. I have been a counseling psychologist for seventeen years now. The lens of counseling can cause us to see the world in a diagnosable/ not-diagnosable framework. I myself have suffered disorders such as addiction illness, periods of depression, and retraumatizing due to my experience as outlined in the Introduction of this book. Forty years of study and contemplation of the human condition, thirty years of recovery, and seventeen years of counseling others have led me to believe that there are not many among us who do not suffer disordering of one sort or another. To recover, our disorders need to be embraced with compassion, with care. Is that not what Jesus modeled in the Gospels, in his healing stories? If one does see samesex love as a disorder, then why not suspend the judgment and treat those who have that disorder with care and compassion? I ask those who would judge and/or condemn, have they ever suffered from depression, anxiety, bipolarity, chemical dependence, or any other of a myriad of disorders? Let those who have suffered no struggle be the first to condemn! Let the rest be silent!

I would also ask those who avoid all critique of human sexual behavior whether there might lurk beneath their non-judgmentalism a reluctance to question their own values and behaviors. "If it feels good, do it," a cheap remnant of the sexual liberation of the sixties, is an attitude that seldom acknowledges the devastation caused to children, the family, and thus the culture when we suspend all judgment about our sexual lifestyles, bothsex or samesex. Do we avoid the psychological, spiritual, and social rigors of maturity when we avoid the difficult work all couples face when choosing to remain together? Is it really true that "it's better for the children" to separate? Is that really true at the species level? Has it any part to play in the epidemic of addiction disorders among our young, leading them to death by overdose, by suicide, by car crashes, and peer murder? Do our young, at the species level, deserve the care, commitment, and concern of both parents? How often is the "I'm okay; you're okay" cliché a refuge used to shirk the legitimate self-analysis required to ascend through the developmental stages that lead to maturity and responsibility? It might be time to drop both conservative and liberal judgmentalism, both right- and left-wing fundamentalism.

It might also be time for those with samesex orientations to acknowledge that DNA and procreation really are at the nucleus of what marriage is. It might be time to stop insisting on the use of language to try to make their special form of love the same thing as marriage if it simply isn't. Could not the samesex community become more creative with regard to naming and sacralizing the samesex form of partnership? Why taunt those who will never be convinced? Instead, why not come up with their own name for union and design sacralizing ritual supports for those unions? Sameness is not equality; differentness with equal value is equality. We are all, in all our varying expressions, the presence of the ChristLogos present eternally and everywhere. Developmental maturity demands of us all to recognize that while we are all different and unique, we are all sentient and all in communion with the divine life community of this planet. Honesty and tolerance must become the core ingredients in our views of each other. Whether conservative or liberal, samesex or bothsex, we are all the embodiment of love. As such, we are all welcome.

Abortion

Again, I assert my request for forbearance and breathing as we walk into the minefield of volatility the abortion issue raises. As noted, I have been counseling for seventeen years at the writing of this book. During that whole time, I have had a "word of mouth" subpractice of healing work with women who have had one, two, and even five abortions. Watching them, sometimes in fetal positions themselves, writhing in agony on my office floor, I have witnessed firsthand what abortion can do to some women. My point is this: I do not write the following from some lofty moral place. I write from the experience of meeting these women in the core of their own personal disasters. The DSM (the Diagnostic and Statistical Manual of the American Psychological Association) editions III, IV, and their successors provide "V-codes" (symptom descriptions) for grief following miscarriage. There are no such codes for those who choose to miscarry, to abort. If a woman does abort and then later, due to a change of or a raising of consciousness, decides that she has "killed her own children," then the earlier, the lower consciousness, who she was then, could not carry the child or did not believe that she could. Her choice might not really have been a choice if she saw no options even if they were there, obvious to those around her. If the body can miscarry because it is not developmentally prepared for pregnancy, then perhaps the psyche can miscarry if it is not developmentally prepared. That latter "miscarriage" is what we call abortion. Developmental stunting can last into the twenties, thirties, forties, and some people truly never grow up.

Life and death are not really opposites, though we often speak as though they are. Birth and death, or more accurately, conception and death, are opposites. Life is the embodied presence of God. As such, it is eternal, nontemporal, and it has no opposite—it just is. Still, the termination of "a life" really is "a death." The in utero being (we have all been one) has no voice and no advocate if his or her mother cannot or does not provide one. The person reading this book must not have been "terminated" prior to birth. All of us who hold whatever opinion about abortion have that one fact in common: none of us were aborted! A unitive position must include *both* the mother and the being in utero in its advocacy. We must transcend the "liberal" advocacy for the mother and the "conservative" advocacy for the in utero child. We must somehow find a way to include both in a transcendent compassion. How?

We humans make many poor choices that often result in sickness and in death. The use of alcohol, drugs, tobacco, automotive reckless-ness, war, pollution, and obesity—these are but a few of the ways we make choices that point toward death. In perhaps every instance, isn't it a level of consciousness or its lack that lurks behind the choice to do so? Those dying of lung cancer often have a different conscious-ness regarding smoking than when they started. Those convicted of vehicular homicide see alcohol abuse in a different light as well. We could say that an unformed and uninformed moral sense was the true cause of the "insanity" of their choices: "If I knew then what I know

now. ...." How many times have we heard it said, or said it ourselves? The unformed and uninformed moral consciousness that leads to pregnancy and abortion could be seen as just such an insanity. Later, a more developmentally mature moral psyche might come to see things differently. Its deeper and wider viewpoint might see options it could not see earlier. The choices made by a higher, more inclusive consciousness would be better choices. Those among us, drunk with hormones, who have never made a bad choice—let those people cast the first condemnation!

Because survival and death really are at stake in abortion, the issue slots easily into our collective bipolar disorder. But at some time, most of us have seen the choice to drink as an advantage, to get high or to divorce as an advantage. So many of these "advantages" end in sickness and in death. We then see our uninformed choices as disordered or insane, and we regret them. In bringing up our daughters, my wife Carol and I made it clear to them that while we would prefer that they abstain from sexual activity and pregnancy until marriage, we would nonetheless welcome both them and their pre-born child into our home. We went further by making it clear that if they felt unable to raise the child, we would, given the opportunity, raise him or her; we agreed to do so even if one of us had already died. Our children thus felt valued and learned the value we felt for their children regardless of their choices or mistakes. We took away the fear that most often drives abortion choices. They were given the safety required in making a real choice—safety for their own person and safety for the personhood of their child. Did we want to begin parenting again in our fifties? No. Would we have done so? Yes! No one is held morally responsible for choices made while being held at gunpoint. Conservative self-righteousness around the right to life (which does in fact appear in the Constitution) and liberal self-righteousness around a woman's right to choose are mirror images of each other. They are both a disservice to us all. Third-millennium Christianity must be a safety net for any pregnant woman regardless of age or circumstances.

Should, at her level of consciousness, she still see abortion as an advantage, we should grieve that choice and still value her. That is unitive compassion and it does not require the court's agreement.

In an ideal world, no one would die from drinking and driving, from drug overdose, or from lung cancer. In an ideal world, all pregnancies would be welcome and all communities, Christian churches in particular, would welcome and support every pregnancy. To welcome and support every pregnancy means to welcome and support every pregnant woman, every newborn, and every child. Because this is not yet the case, we are left with this volatile and difficult issue. Liberals champion a woman's right to choose. The moral roots for this assertion lie in the Judeo-Christian prophetic tradition. Because both Hebrew and Roman cultures saw women as property, the prophets cried out for their protection. In our time, in order to protect this "right" the Supreme Court ruled that the in utero being is not a person in the legal sense, and therefore not entitled to protection by law. Conservatives, hearing an echo from Auschwitz in this, asserted that the child in utero is a person in the "spiritual sense," a sense that precedes the legal sense in time and in authority. They, however, then turned on women having abortions, calling some of them murderers. Further, those children in utero who do survive the "choice" of parents are more often welcomed into life and supported by social programs guaranteed by liberals. The born child does not always receive these post-birth supports from the conservatives. While those same conservatives deny Darwinian evolution, they nonetheless frequently assert an implied social Darwinism post-birth in a "survival of the fittest" political agenda. Survival of the fittest better translates into survival of the richest. Again, to welcome every pregnancy means welcome for every woman, every newborn, and every child. Welcome means bearing the cost of hospitality as individuals and as communities and cultures. Less than this *cannot* be called Christian!

In the United States, about three million abortions occur annually. Three million times a year, choices are made perhaps by unformed or uninformed moral consciousnesses that involve directly nine million people, counting mothers, fathers, and in utero children. That's a lot of grief, anguish, and shame floating among us every year! However we view it, six million people have lacked the moral maturity and development to make good choices regarding their sexual behaviors and corresponding responsibilities. Meanwhile, the culture holds up its corporate and Hollywood "heroes"—grotesque caricatures of adulthood, narcissists driven to hysteria and wallowing in money—as role models for our young people. The religious establishment hasn't done much better in providing alternatives. What we value is what our children will become in their attempt to please us. Disposable marriages, disposable children, disposable pregnancies, disposable ecosystems, and disposable nations are required in our mad and narcissistic gluttony. The need to raise our consciousness has become an issue of cultural and even planetary survival. We have the information to support the growth of our moral psyches. We need the transformation individually and collectively to make it real. Ingredients from both science and global culture will enable us to do so.

While it is truly difficult to see partial birth abortion as anything other than infanticide, I am sure there are instances that challenge that perception. This is actually, in my opinion, also true for many if not most third-trimester abortions in that, generally speaking, the fetuses are viable. Creating language in an attempt to disguise that which is obvious to anyone is a disservice to everyone. It creates more rage, more madness. Consider the following: (1) If a woman suffers a miscarriage at any point in pregnancy, she is supported in her grief over the loss of her "baby"; (2) if she chooses to "terminate" her pregnancy, her "fetus" would be removed and disposed of by the medical establishment; (3) if on the way to the women's clinic to get an abortion she is killed by a drunk driver, that person is guilty of a double homicide, the killing of two "people"; (4) or, should she give birth and the next day for whatever reason kill her "baby," then she is charged with murder; (5) or, if the "baby" is born prematurely, the same medical establishment that might have "terminated" the pregnancy yesterday and disposed of the "fetus" would then prescribe millions in life supports to save the "baby's" life. Is this not insanity? Does this not indicate our deep and truly schizoid confusion regarding procreation and life? Does an infant become a partial-birth fetus when we change its name? Does a fetus become a baby when we choose to allow it to live? Does a baby become a fetus if we choose to abort? Does a woman experience less grief from losing a baby by miscarriage than by abortion? Must we disenfranchise mother, preborn child, or born child? Truly, what in *hell* is going on? Either no one is at fault, or we all are! We must transcend into decency and include in compassion all that lives, born and reborn. We must inform ourselves and transform our world into a higher consciousness.

Education and not condemnation is the way through to transcendence and higher ordering. Documentaries such as *In the Womb* by the National Geographic Society can teach us more than an army of conservative or liberal moralists. Were it shown in every church, temple, and school for a year, abortion numbers would tumble from millions to hundreds of thousands. Show it and others like it for a decade, and abortions would come down to the thousands. And for those thousands, the woman "choosing" the abortions would receive the compassion of our hospitals rather than abandonment to back-alley charlatans. Or we can choose to defend our bipolar ideologies and increase the general madness. In any case, we choose!

So, if we are to find a unitive position, we must improve our unitive welcome. One way to begin is to welcome the moral teachings of all religious traditions to be taught as history courses in all our primary and secondary schools. The materials are among us and should simply be presented as history and/or geography. Pagan, agnostic, and atheist positions must be included in these "moral history" courses. The young people would at least be given the raw materials needed for moral development. Second, we must welcome our children and their pregnancies without shame or condemnation—and with the full support of social services that provide the safety needed for real choice. Third, we must allow safe and clean hospital abortions for those unable to see an alternative at any given point. We must accept their "choice" as, more often than not, a psychic miscarriage; they would make better choices if they could. Their psychic miscarriage grief should be equally validated alongside physical miscarriage grief, and all insurance carriers should be forced by law to fund counseling services. Fourth, all judgments and/or condemnations must be withdrawn. No child is "illegitimate" or "born out of wedlock"; each child is a child. Every child is a presentation of the ChristLogos, and the ChristLogos is never illegitimate. Let's remember, the child Jesus was conceived to an unwed mother. Fifth, all children must be entitled to all social services because all children are our children. Last, we must forgive each other's conservative and liberal judgmentalism. We, all of us, are those whom he forgave because we never really know what it is we are doing.

CHAPTER 30

Forgiving Christianity

"Forgive them, for they know not what they do." When Jesus uttered these words from his cross of agony, what was he really saying? He was saying, "Forgive them their insanity." One never has to look too far to be confronted with the same insanity. Two days ago, thirty-two people were gunned down in Virginia by an insane person before he made himself the thirty-third. No small amount of the insanity handed down to us, beaten into us, comes from distorted religious teachings. As I noted in the Introduction, Christianity has certainly been no exception to this. As noted over and over again throughout this book, both right- and left-wing fundamentalisms continue the ego-driven tug of war that flays and tears the body of Christ. The world of the ego, individually and collectively, strives always to announce its uniqueness, separateness, and rightness. The brain-bound mind is always right there—all three voices justifying the madness.

The consciousness of the fourth voice, the ChristLogos, transforms the brain, forcing it to think with the mind of Christ. Through that lens, available to all, the brain-bound ego-voice is clearly the voice of insanity. Jesus, the man of sorrows, arrived at Golgotha understanding the real meaning of his journey. But for the one moment of doubt due to the horror of his pain, he became firmly embedded in a higher mind. His thoughts no longer screamed "What about me? What about me?" His feelings no longer fed up to his mind the self-pity he must have struggled with. His instincts no longer screamed signals about self-survival. His brain, transformed by realization and by suffering, was able to accommodate the unitive mind, the fourth voice. His identity was no longer Jesus of Nazareth but the ChristLogos. What earlier might have been a response of disgust or revulsion for the grinning and demented stupidities of human existence had now become in his unitive view the object of his compassion. The ugly hate-twisted faces who didn't even know why they called for his crucifixion were now transparent to him. He could see his own self, the ChristLogos, within each of them. Responding to the beauty they ran from in themselves, he could love them and thus forgive them.

During my lifetime, Christianity as a whole seems to have done away with Christ's message about our inherent value. The churches have peddled guilt, shame, and fallen-ness in order to avoid the joy present in our deepest, our real, nature. Guilt and shame have often been useful tools in assuring that the "faithful" would continue in their dependence upon an unenlightened hierarchy who neither entered into joy nor allowed others to enter in. These people either did not share the truth of our real, our divine, nature with the "faithful" or they were simply ignorant of it themselves. In any case, in my experience, the joy and love by which Jesus wanted his followers to be recognized have often been displaced by the emotional acid of guilt and shame or the pretense of some near-hysterical acting out of joy. Along with the guilt and shame, there was always the promise of being expunged of guilt and shame, if only the guilty and the shameful could find the right formula. That formula, held by the hierarchy of the ordained, "entrusted to them by God," seemed always just out of reach. What becomes obvious in spiritual maturity, with its attendant spiritual authority, is that few if any of the ordained have had any real sense of what Jesus actually meant. And look out if genuine authority did emerge in you! Lacking it themselves, they knew just how to crush it in the faithful: guilt and shame!

Michael was a student of mine in a Catholic high school here in New Hampshire. He was sixteen or seventeen years old when he was in my World Religions class. He's the kid who never got a B. When he received his dual master's degree in theology and social work, he was still getting straight As. Nor was he the nerd type. A fine athlete and handsome, he was loved by the guys as well as the girls. Following his master's and deeply called by Christ, he began a ministry to people in the streets of Rochester, New York. He's about to turn forty presently, has been married to one woman, has two twin pre-teenagers, and is still with the people of the streets. He belonged to a "Catholic" parish that became radically inclusive about samesex couples and the poor. Warned by the bishop to "tone it down" (the Sanhedrin had the same advice for Jesus), his parishioners refused the bishop's advice. The whole parish, priest and all, were ex-communicated from the Catholic fold. They continued together as a parish, and ten or so years later are vibrant and growing as a community. Michael is respected as an elder and is much sought after as a preacher—and is still in the streets with the poor. Are we *really* to believe that Michael is cast out of Christ's love and concern because some bishop pronounces it so? The ridiculous should be ridiculed. Ridicule strips away pretentious claims to authority. Dante had a special place for such bishops!

As noted in the Introduction, I was forced out of the Catholic communion by my own trauma when the news broke about the sexual crisis of the early 1990s. I had been at daily mass for twenty-five years, was trained by the Benedictines in theology, and was a somewhat prominent Catholic. To this day, I have heard from no one, except for the bishop of Manchester. I suspected at the time that he was comforting himself by "going after the lost sheep," but I agreed to meet him at a local college. The reason I refused to meet him at diocesan corporate headquarters is that I had never stepped into that building without later emerging feeling trivialized, diminished, and shamed. So we met. We had a period of three hours earmarked for our time together. The night before, I did a deep surrender to God, expressing my willingness to go back to the Catholic communion if that was God's will for me. My only request was that he make it clear to me what I was to do. When we were together, I told the bishop the whole story of my abuse from the fourth to the eleventh grades. When the good bishop fell asleep for the third time, recalling the first apostle's behavior in the garden of Jesus' agony, I realized that God's will was indeed made clear. I said goodbye to the bishop and we parted. About a month later, I felt pulled to go to this small Episcopal church in Peterborough, which my wife Carol and I had attended during our courtship. We've been there ever since with rectors Adrian and Sarah Robbins-Cole. Episcopal Christianity has been my first experience of welcome and inclusion in the Christian community. The first of my life! The ridiculous deserve to be ridiculed! Or do they? Perhaps they should be forgiven their insanity, for they know not what they do?

In speaking of the sexual molestation crisis, it is important to comment on the collusion and cowardice of so many local churchgoers in the midst of the exposed agonies of their fellows. As I mentioned, after near-daily attendance at Eucharist for twenty-five years, not one person to date has, prompted by their own concern, contacted me about my disappearance from "the community." Clearly, community is not the right word! Some have passed me in the supermarket and pretended not to know me. I had friends who nervously explained to me that they couldn't imagine separation from the sacraments. One actually said, "Who will bury me?" This from the "disciple" of the teacher who said, "Leave the dead to bury their dead"! To continue in a co-dependent and fear-based allegiance to an institution while those around you are devastated by the same institution is collusion, and collusion is the product of cowardice. When the "Christian" church exhibits the very disorders diagnosed by Jesus in Judaism, it is time for all members to withdraw financial support and demand change.

Fearing the loss of career or of pensions, the priests and bishops just go on even when their real careers are already over by virtue of just going on. Fearing the damnation they have been taught will accompany separation from the sacraments, the fearful go on. Meanwhile, the victims whose lives have been permanently distorted are retraumatized by this collusion of those around them and are forced to walk alone with their agonies. Only the strongest among them will ever arrive at the same realization that Jesus had: "Forgive them their insanity, for they know not what they are doing." When he spoke those words, he forgave all the Jews and all the Romans for all time. He grasped the hideous distortions of the egoic self—their blindness, their deafness, and their utter insanity. He understood their complete lack of culpability due to the insanity. Forgiveness happens when we accept responsibility for the internal hurts we have borne and no longer expect anyone to heal them. Forgiveness happens when disgust is transmuted into compassion.

But the distortions radiate outward in larger circles of damage, to include biocide and even ecocide. The damage to the life community, while perhaps not completely encouraged by the Christian institution, has at least been tolerated and seldom confronted in any meaningful way. For twenty centuries, we have prayed to a creator God responsible for the being of the planet and the life community. We have prayed to the Holy Spirit, the "Lord and Giver of Life." Meanwhile, the clergy have too often snuggled up to their corporate and governmental counterparts. Seldom have they made meaningful comment while the same Earth and her creatures have been destroyed. Jesus warned of "he that could destroy both body and soul." The biocidal and ecocidal misuse of the Earth is that very destruction of both body and soul—the body through a hundred forms of cancer and other disorders, the soul through the exile of beauty, meaning, and hope. The despair moves among us like one of the plagues of Egypt. Egocentricity, both individual and collective, is the very insanity Jesus was attempting to forgive.

As already mentioned, those who abuse children and are representatives of any religious establishment abuse not only the bodies but the souls of their victims. Children do not yet have the sophistication needed to differentiate those who represent God and the God they represent. Therefore, their experience is that God is abusing them. My physical abuse ended at age fifteen when I discovered I had the ability to end it at school and at home. As I finish this book, I have just turned sixty. Like most victims, I have spent forty-five years recovering from the injuries—theological, cognitive, affective, instinctual, and sexual—that result from the desecration of abuse. Only those who have been hurt in that way seem to understand the depth of that kind of injury. Still, one remains a victim for only so long as one denies oneself what is needed in order to recover. As noted, Jesus left us the model of transcendence into compassion. In my case, the working out of my own understanding of Christianity and experiential knowledge of Christ has brought me to the writing of this book and the ability to announce that very forgiveness.

Jesus was asked how many times one should forgive. He reported on that occasion that *if asked,* one should forgive seventy times seven times, or what comes to 490 times. The horrible truth, at least in my experience, is that there has been no genuine request for forgiveness. Nor has there even been an unequivocal recognition of the true dimensions of the vast crime against children who have now grown into adults. Nevertheless, I myself have arrived at forgiveness. The true grandeur of Christianity, and the true significance of Christ, are unaltered by the myopic, cowardly, and infantile distortions by those who coopt its ownership. I want to make it clear that I forgive the 490 times I have been wounded by the infliction and retraumatizing of woundings by those who called themselves sisters, brothers, and fathers. I also forgive the collusion of those who, avoiding inconvenience to themselves, avoid a genuine acknowledgment of what all of this has really meant. I forgive the insane teachers and the insanity they marketed in the name of Christ. I forgive the absurdities of all fundamentalisms, Catholic or otherwise.

And while I do forgive them, I shall never again feign respect for that which is not respectable. Never again will I be silent in the face of perversion and distortion. Many are too infantile, too adolescent to do the real work of growing up. Instead, they often hide in institutions and demand respect while they injure those in their care and attack those who would question their hegemony—those they call "heretics" or "new-agers" or whatever else. Jesus did not shrink from calling Herod a fox or calling religious professionals dens of snakes and tombs filled with rot. He did not shrink from reminding Pilate that his powers were not his own. I forgive those who abuse Christian truth for political ends, who have little or no compassion for the poor and the vulnerable, or for those creatures with whom we share this planet. I forgive those who turn Christianity on its head by serving the wealthy, themselves first and foremost among them. I forgive them all seven hundred times seven times. But never again will I be silent. I know him who dwells within me; I *AM* him who dwells within me. And whether or not you realize it, so are you!

By Rev. Sarah Robbins-Cole

Christianity, Incarnation, and Yoga: Unifying Faith, Religion, and Practice

> So God created humankind in his image, in the image of God he created them, male and female he created them. … God saw everything that he had made, and indeed, it was very good. And there was evening and there was morning, the sixth day.
>
> GENESIS 1:27, 31

> And the word became flesh and lived among us, and we have seen his glory, the glory as of a father's only son, full of grace and truth.
>
> JOHN 1:14

The Theology

Dr. LaChance highlights in this book the ways in which the modern Christian mystic can seek not only unifying understanding of the world around him- or herself, but a way of experiencing it. This unitive approach most certainly resonates with my own life of faith as well as my work, not only as an Episcopal priest but also a yoga teacher. This unifying principle is akin to what is said in Chapter 5, Life: The Sacrament of the Earth, namely, if God chose to become a primate, then who are we to disdain our origins?

For me, this unitive approach finds its source in the starting point of Christianity, the Incarnation—the coming of God in human form so that God may be comprehended in a new and meaningful way. The Incarnation invites humanity to find out the true nature of God by beholding something we can recognize: a human form. If you want to know the will of God, what matters to God most, what the nature of God is, look to the actions and words of Jesus of Nazareth—the complete manifestation of divinity and humanity in a single, unitive being.

Jesus teaches us a multiplicity of things, but the most important is that our lives are about loving "the Lord your God with all your heart, and with all your soul, and with all your mind; and your neighbor as yourself." Jesus also teaches us the importance of being involved in the healing of the world through healing, feeding, clothing, and visiting those in need.

This command to love God and love our neighbor, and the ethical command to take care of those in need around us teaches us that God has created us for a purpose and has given us a body to carry out these actions. Likewise, the care of the body, mind, and soul of others is further confirmation that the body is important. This all culminates in the ultimate appreciation of the body in the resurrection and subsequent ascension of Jesus in bodily form, and the promise of our own bodily resurrection.

We do not need to look only in the Christian scriptures to find this affirmation. Far earlier, in the Hebrew Scriptures, the person who put the creation story into written form tells us that God is pleased with every step of creation. In fact, God is recorded as saying that each step along the way is "good." However, there is an important and distinct declaration after the creation of humans: God sees what God has created and claims it as "very good."

This sense of good can be seen in two lights. First, there was a qualitative appreciation of what was created. But more important, and perhaps more accurate, God sees that human form will fulfill a purpose, in the sense that it will achieve the ends (or the good) that God wishes for that form to fulfill. In Dr. LaChance's terms, God has created a being that can carry out the "politics of decency."

The goodness of creation and the goodness of flesh, or the body, is at the heart of my faith and that is a faith I share with most Christians. However, Christianity has not always been seen to embrace this aspect of bodily goodness, largely because of imports from other religious and philosophical beliefs, namely, Gnosticism and Neo-Platonism. It is also the Christian belief that we live in a fallen world, where we are made in the image of God, but sometimes we make choices that result in treating our bodies badly as well as the body of what we often call "mother Earth" even when we know better. In the words of St. Paul: "For I do not do what I want, but I do the very thing I hate" (Romans 7:15). Despite our fallen-ness, Christianity, with God's inherent desire and Jesus' teaching, demands that its followers respect the body and be good stewards of the earth, and when we do not, to turn and repent and start anew.

The Religion

I am grateful every day that this theology, this faith, was made into an institution. Despite the modern age's tendency to loath all things institutional, without the institution, or in fact St. Paul's dogma and passion, Christianity would probably have not made it thus far.

Early on, at the beginning of the institution of Christianity, the religion continued to value the body, most profoundly in the sacraments, as discussed in Dr. LaChance's chapters on the sacraments. In the sacrament of the Eucharist, Jesus becomes incarnate in the bread and wine; they become the body and blood of Christ. We celebrate the flesh of Jesus and its spiritual and healing properties when we come forward and receive communion. Jesus said, "I am the living bread which came down from heaven; if any one eats of this bread, he will live for ever; and the bread which I shall give for the life of the world is my flesh."

The sacrament of Baptism celebrates the new bodily life of a child who has come into the world to love, worship, and serve God. And even in the case of adult baptism, the person who is baptized is starting a new life—body, mind, and soul, given over to the purposes of Father, Son, and Holy Spirit.

Even Paul, for all the criticism that he receives rightly or wrongly, presents positive imagery of the body. Two examples come to mind. First, the Church is made analogous to "one body with many members." Paul urges the Corinthians to consider their health as the body of Christ depends on them all valuing one another and seeing themselves as the incarnation of Christ together. In Paul's words: "For in the one Spirit we were all baptized into the one body—Jews or Greeks, slaves or free—and we were all made to drink of one spirit" (I Corinthians 12:13). The second example is Paul's insistence that the body be respected. He writes: "Do you not know that your body is a temple of the Holy Spirit within you, which you have from God, and that you are not your own? You were bought with a price; therefore glorify God in your body" (I Corinthians 19:20). In a sense, if the Holy Spirit is going to reside in the body, the body must be taken care of so that is a good receptacle, not filled with toxins and poisons, and kept, to the best of our abilities and age, in the best shape that it can be.

The Practice

I have been an Episcopal priest for twelve years, a yogi for about nine years, and a yoga teacher for four years. Although Christianity had provided me with a way to quench my intellectual life, met my desire to worship, and attended to my theological curiosities, my unitive whole was not being engaged. Episcopalians often pride themselves on being the denomination where you do not need to check your brain at the door. It has often felt more like the body is the part of the whole that we divorce ourselves from. It is true that my body is used as a vehicle to get me to church and to stand, kneel, stand, genuflect, bow, and cross myself, but my body was not utilized in my faith in a holistic way. Before I entered seminary I was a body person—a runner, skier, and hiker. In seminary and in the church, these things were merely extra-curricular activities.

But when I moved to England, and was first ordained, I joined a gym that offered yoga. I did not know anything about yoga except being attracted to its practice as a child watching a woman named Joanie teaching yoga on PBS. When I started taking classes, that feeling of coming home occurred immediately. I took more classes and practiced more regularly, and then started a yoga teacher training program. The course I trained on encouraged the study of philosophy and the eight-limbed path of yoga. At the same time I was teaching comparative religions at a boy's school in London, where I was the school chaplain. As I learned more about yoga and more about Hinduism, the more I began to see a way to practice Christianity emerging. Did I feel conflicted about what appears to be syncretism? Not at all. As Dr. LaChance writes in Chapter 6, Culture: The Sacrament of Life, namely, that mysticism unites us with an experience that transcends language and culture. Surely, if this is the case, then why not share good practice?

What has emerged for me is a spiritual checklist of practices that I have taken from Hinduism and yoga and, in a sense, "Christianized" them for my own use. It makes good sense to use yoga for a number of reasons. First, yoga is often claimed to be a philosophy and not a religion so that it is flexible in its adaptation to other world religions. Second, the aim of yoga is to yoke or join the practitioner into union with the source of all being, God, and in that union, join the practitioner with all of the universe. There are four main types of yoga, and although each path individually can lead you to God, I find that the combination of the four helps me to feel balanced and whole.

Bhakti yoga is the yoga of love and devotion through worship. Hindu families would follow this path through worship in their homes and in a *mandir* (a place of worship, a temple). For me, it is the recitation of the daily offices at home, and the Eucharist and other liturgical services in church. I also try throughout my day to worship God through the constant awareness of my immense gratitude for the life that I have been given, the people in my life, the Earth, and for the talents, time, and money God has graciously given to me as a steward of those abundant gifts. When I cease to worship daily, it is harder to see the grace of God around me.

Jnana yoga is the joining of man to God, or self-realization, through knowledge. In Hinduism this would mean the study of scripture and philosophy. For me, this is the study of God through books on spirituality, philosophy, theology, and scripture. The more I read and reflect on my reading the more I feel I know about God; consequently, I feel closer to God. When I do not read, my mind becomes stale and sluggish.

Karma yoga is the joining of humanity to God, or the path to enlightenment, through good works. Karma yoga is the way of action, of responding to need without thought of reward. Karma yoga feels like the yoga of the Epistle of James in the New Testament: "For just as the body without spirit is dead, so faith without works is also dead" (James 2:26). Good works are not only a sign of faith, but also a way to faith. That is, the more loving and compassionate I am to the world around me, the closer to God I feel. Another by-product, is that I feel closer to the world around me too. The shroud of individualism is worn away by good acts done in the name of Christ. Without good, thoughtful actions, the mind finds an opportunity to hold fast to selfish, egotistical thinking and desires.

The final form of yoga is *raja* yoga, which also can subsume *hatha* yoga, the physical yoga. Raja yoga is primarily the form of yoga that creates a union between God and the practitioner through meditation. One of the first steps to getting the body to cooperate with that mission is the exercise and stretching of the body in the form of hatha yoga. While practicing yoga is not a form of meditation, it does have a meditative quality about it. The necessity to concentrate and focus on what one is doing with the body during practice brings the quality of stillness and focus to body, mind, and soul. In some Christian circles yoga is used as prayer. Various asanas (positions) are put together in a flow of movements and set to words such as the Lord's Prayer or music.

The faith of Christianity is said to be in the heart. The religion of Christianity is preserved and taught in the institution so that faith may be informed and nurtured. And the practice of Christianity is found in the daily life of the believer. For me, that path has been made easier through the study of yoga which has led me to daily worship, study, acts of compassion and kindness, and the use of my body, mind, and soul in the physical practice of hatha yoga and the subsequent stilling of the body, mind, and soul in meditation. The experience of studying yoga brought a richness, a wholeness to my Christian faith. Dr. LaChance speaks of the profound impact of T. S. Eliot's *Four Quartets* on his own spiritual journey. I share that experience with him. Yoga brought me to a place that Eliot described as where we arrive at where we started, but know that place for the first time.

But even without the paths of yoga, I *know,* because God created our human bodies, and Jesus is God made flesh, that when I use my body to run, ski, walk my dog, or carry my children, God smiles, because I am doing the thing that is what we all want done when we give a gift, to see it used and appreciated.

About the Author

Albert J. LaChance, PhD, LADC, CAS, has written and spoken widely on the subjects of spirituality, psychology, ecology, and addiction. From 1990 to the present, he has run Greenspirit: The Center for Counseling and Consciousness, in Manchester, New Hampshire, where he counsels individuals, families, and groups, and has consulted organizations regarding interpersonal dynamics. His agency presently focuses on psychological evaluations and expert witness work for the courts, as well as offering spiritual guidance and mentoring. Prior to this, he worked with Thomas Berry for five years at his Riverdale Center for Religious Research. Dr. LaChance is an American Academy certified Addiction Specialist in the areas of sex addiction and chemical dependency. He is a member of the National Association of Alcohol and Drug Counselors. He is also a licensed Addictions Counselor in the state of New Hampshire and has received training as a Domestic Violence counselor.

Dr. LaChance has authored several books, the most recent being *Cultural Addiction: The Greenspirit Guide to Recovery,* published by North Atlantic Books in 2006. The original edition, entitled *Greenspirit: Twelve Steps in Ecological Spirituality,* represented a major contribution to the fields of psychology, spirituality, and ecology when it was first published fifteen years earlier. In *The Architecture of the Soul: A Unitive Model of the Human Person,* published in 2005, Dr. LaChance draws from a wide range of disciplines and philosophies, to present a model of the human person that can be used for interpreting and treating human dysfunction. Other books he has written include *Embracing Earth: Catholic Approaches to Ecology* (co-authored with John E.

Carroll) and *Jonah: A Prophecy at the Millennium,* a 1,400-line mystical poem springing from the work of T. S. Eliot. Dr. LaChance has also contributed chapters to *The Other Half of My Soul: Bede Griffiths and the Hindu-Christian Dialogue* (edited by Beatrice Bruteau), *The Greening of Faith: God, the Environment, and the Good Life* (edited by John E. Carroll, Paul Brockelman, and Mary Westfall), and *Sister Earth: Ecology and the Spirit* (by Dom Helder Camara), for which he wrote the introduction.

Dr. LaChance has taught world religions from high school through to the graduate level, at several colleges, including the University of New Hampshire, New England College, and Granite State College. He has spoken nationally for Cross Country University on the topics of sex addiction, and psychology and spirituality, and has conducted numerous local workshops. He teaches a monthly course on Christian Mysticism at All Saints Parish in Peterborough, New Hampshire, and has recently offered a guided retreat on mysticism for members of the Unitarian Church in Seattle, Washington. He has also been interviewed widely on television and radio, in newspapers, and in magazines. Dr. LaChance continues to write, counsel, teach, and speak on all the above topics.

2482

10/6